MC

NOTES

ncluding
- *Introduction*
- *Brief Summary*
- *Chapter Summaries and Discussions*
- *Critical Analysis*
- *Character Sketches*
- *Study Questions*
- *Bibliography*

)y
Nancy Levi Arnez, Ed.D.

INCORPORATED

LINCOLN, NEBRASKA   68501

Editor

Consulting Editor

Gary Carey, M.A.
University of Colorado

James L. Roberts, Ph.D.
Department of English
University of Nebraska

ISBN 0-8220-0854-8
© Copyright 1969
by
C. K. Hillegass
All Rights Reserved
Printed in U.S.A.

1992 Printing

Cliffs Notes, Inc.   Lincoln, Nebraska

CONTENTS

INTRODUCTION

Early Life

One of three children, Daniel Defoe was born to James Foe, a butcher, and his wife Alice, in the parish of St. Giles, Cripplegate, London about 1660. It seems that Defoe's name went through various spellings: Foe, Faugh, DuFoo, Du'Foe, DeFoe, DeFooe, Dukow (a sexton's error) and Daniel Defoe, Esq. Often Defoe signed himself D.F., D.D.F. or D.Foe.

James Foe was of middle-class stock, although his mother was apparently higher-born. Despite this, Defoe lived his early years in poverty and hardship because of the political and religious views of his father, a pious Dissenter from the Church of England and follower of Oliver Cromwell.

When Defoe was five or six years old, two appalling events occurred which deeply affected him: the Plague and the Great Fire of London. In his later writings he vividly describes both events. and presents a particularly unforgettable picture of them in his *Journal of the Plague Year* (1722).

Because his father was a Dissenter, Daniel was denied the privilege of attending either Oxford or Cambridge. Nevertheless, dissenting academies had been established in various parts of the country. It was to one of these, Stoke Newington Academy, kept by Charles Morton, that Defoe was sent when he was ten years old to prepare for the Presbyterian ministry. He attended the academy from 1674 to 1679 and learned there science and the humanities. Latin, however, was not taught, an omission which Daniel regretted all his life for he felt every learned man should have a command of that language. Morton lectured in English and required his boys to write in their native language. It was under Mr. Morton's tutelage that Daniel learned to write in the clear colloquial style he is known for.

5

An Introduction to Business

After four years at the academy, Daniel decided against becoming a minister and turned his attention to the business world. This was a time when the tempo of business was quickening. In two or three years fortunes were being made on the Exchange which would take forty years to amass in a small business. The London merchant was gaining a foothold in the economy of the country because of the rapid increase of trade. It was during the 1680's that the modern business world was born. Defoe became an apprentice to a hosiery merchant and two years later he became a haberdasher with a shop in a high-rent district in the heart of London.

The Pamphleteer

In 1683 he published his first political pamphlet. One year later on January 1, 1684, he married Mary Tuffley, who brought him a dowry of £3,700. The couple had seven children during their forty-seven years of married life.

In 1685, Defoe became involved in the Duke of Monmouth's fight to take the throne of England from his uncle, James Stuart. James, a Catholic, not only opposed religious freedom for Protestants, but tried to establish the precept of divine right of kings over his fellow Roman Catholics.

Between 1687–88 several tracts of protest against the King are attributed to Defoe. Shortly thereafter, Defoe spent some time traveling on the Continent where he won the favor of William of Orange who subsequently invaded England in 1688 and forced James Stuart into exile in France. He held several minor offices under William and served as his confidant and advisor. Most of the thirty-six books and tracts he published during William's reign supported the King's policies.

Bankruptcy

Business now became Defoe's main interest. In January, 1688, he was admitted as a liveryman to the City of London. He became a merchant and was beginning to prosper when war broke out with France in 1692 and trade was severely interrupted. Defoe was forced into bankruptcy and it took him ten years to pay off all but £5,000 of the original £17,000 debt incurred.

More Political Maneuverings

His first book, *An Essay Upon Projects,* was published in 1698. It set forth his views on road building and maintenance, labor, banks, insurance, income tax, friendly societies, asylums for idiots, academies, and schools for women.

William of Orange was not a popular ruler among the English because he was Dutch. Defoe, however, admired the King who, like Defoe, believed in ideas like religious tolerance, union between England and Scotland, and expansion of English trade. As an outgrowth of his admiration for William, who was foreign-born, Defoe wrote a satirical poem, "The True-Born Englishman." It showed how the English population was actually composed of many different races and nationalities. This poem won favor among the populace but was viewed with disfavor by the Tories.

When William died in 1702, Defoe fell from favor. During the reign of William, the Dissenters had enjoyed a period of relative peace, but with the accession of Anne, they were again persecuted. Matters for Defoe were not improved when he anonymously published *The Shortest Way With the Dissenters,* a satirical piece which inflamed Tories and Whigs alike because both misinterpreted it. His authorship was soon discovered and a warrant for his arrest was issued charging him with high crimes and misdemeanors. Defoe absconded but soon surrendered and was convicted. He was put into Newgate Prison where he remained for three months gathering impressions, many of which he later used in his books. After three months, Defoe was put in the pillory for three days where he fared quite well at the hands of the mob, who might have at last understood the true meaning of his satiric piece. An outcome of this experience in the pillory was a poem titled *Hymn to the Pillory.*

With Defoe's imprisonment, business at his tile factory at Tilbury declined and his family became destitute. Seemingly a bargain was struck up between Defoe and Robert Harley, a rising Tory politician who was Speaker of the House of Parliament. By forcing Defoe to remain in prison for several months after his experience on the pillory and then securing his release at a strategic moment of despair, he bought Defoe's loyalty for Queen Anne.

With Harley's backing, Defoe began publishing a news-paper entitled *The Review* in 1704. It continued to be published for seven years, much of the time as an organ for the Tory Government.

In 1706 Defoe went to Scotland as a secret-service agent for Harley in an effort to cement relations between England and Scotland. His protracted stay in Scotland was explained as a means for him to further his business interests and later as a means to research facts in order to write a history of the union, which he did finally publish in 1709. About two years after he left, when the union between Scotland and England was accomplished, he returned to England.

Harley fell from power in 1708, shortly after Defoe's return from Scotland. Defoe then switched his loyalty to Sidney Godolphin, Harley's successor, and tried to switch back when Harley returned to power as Chancellor of the Exchequer in 1710. During this time there was some strain between the two men,which became apparent when Defoe lost favor in 1713 and was replaced by Jonathan Swift, another pamphleteer.

An unhappy man with waning fortunes, Defoe moved his family to a home in Stoke Newington, where he continued to publish *The Review*, in which he expressed his horror at the suggestion of bringing back the exiled Stuarts after the anticipated death of the ailing Queen Anne. His quick publication of three pamphlets dealing with the Succession led to his arrest on April 11, 1713 at his house in Newington and subsequent imprisonment in Newgate. He was freed shortly thereafter when he paid his bail. On November 20th he received a pardon signed by Bolingbroke on behalf of the Queen.

June 11, 1713, saw the end of *The Review* which had out-lived its usefulness because of Defoe's constant switches from the Whigs to the Tories. He now began writing for the *Mercator* which appeared regularly until July 20, 1714.

After Queen Anne's death in July, 1714, George I became King of England. On August 28th Defoe was again arrested because of a libelous letter which he had supposedly written for the *Flying Post*. This situation revealed his shady involvement with the printer of the *Flying Post*, William Hurt, who continued to print the paper in conjunction with Defoe even though the owner fired him and hired another printer. Thus readers found themselves confronted with two papers of the same name. In 1715 Defoe was brought to trial and found guilty. Sentence was deferred until the following term and seemingly it was completely withheld, for in September of the same year Defoe became more active than ever before in political journalism, writing numerous tracts and contributing to numerous newspapers and other periodicals. He was also secretly in the service of the Whigs while openly known as a Tory.

On July 12, 1715, Robert Harley, Earl of Oxford, was impeached and brought to the Tower. In this same year Defoe published *The Family Instructor,* a series of moral dialogues of instruction between parents and children, husband and wives, masters and servants.

Harley was in prison for two years before a date was set for his trial. On a petition from Harley himself, his trial date was set for June 24, 1717. Just one day prior to the trial, a volume was published titled, *Minutes of the Negociations of Mons. Mesnager at the Court of England, Towards the Close of the Last Reign,* which, if a true account, would prove Harley not guilty of the charges on which he was about to stand trial. Many believed the *Minutes* were written by Defoe in an effort to save Harley, but Defoe repeatedly denied this. Shortly after this episode, Defoe wrote for Nathaniel Mist's *Journal* in support of the Tories while secretly writing for the opposition Whig Journal, *Mercurius Britannicus.* It was not until 1724 that his political deception was discovered by Mist, at which time the two men had a fight. Neither was seriously hurt but their collaboration was at an end.

The Novelist

In 1719 Defoe wrote *Robinson Crusoe,* which opened the way for a new literary form which was able to reach a new reading public consisting of the middle and lower classes. The novel was supposedly based on the adventures of Alexander Selkirk, whom Defoe had met personally.

After *Robinson Crusoe* came other narratives, among them *Captain Singleton* in 1720, *Moll Flanders* in 1722, *Colonel Jack* in 1722, *Memoirs of a Cavalier* in 1724 and *Roxana* in 1724. Meanwhile, Defoe continued writing his pamphlets and news articles while also engaging himself in numerous business ventures.

Defoe continued writing until 1728. During that same year he was harrassed by Mary Brooke for a debt that he had long since thought settled. To escape this harrassment and possible loss of property and fortune, he took lodging in a rooming house in Ropemaker's Alley, where he died at age 70 on April 26, 1731. Defoe was subsequently buried in Bunhill Fields under the name "Mr. Dubow," a misspelling by the gravedigger.

BRIEF SUMMARY OF THE NOVEL

Moll Flanders is a story about the fall and rise of a beautiful woman who was born in Newgate Prison. Because of her determination to be someone other than a servant, and because of her great greed, she sought to marry a wealthy man. She married some with money and some without. One of her husbands, she learned to her horror, was her brother, by whom she had several children. Her fear of poverty led her to commit many criminal acts. However, even when she had obtained a large store of cash and goods, she continued stealing.

Her ingenious disguises helped her evade prison for many years, in spite of the fact that a number of her accomplices were caught and hanged or transported to the colonies. Moll's heart hardened as she continued to escape arrest. Greed drove her on until she became known as the richest thief in London. Her "governess," who was at one time Moll's midwife, became her partner-in-crime and guided her criminal activities. She later grew penitent and devout and remained Moll's loyal friend for many years.

When Moll became less cautious, she was finally captured and taken to Newgate Prison where she was taunted by the other prisoners. Moll repented momentarily as she confessed her crimes to her spiritual adviser, a minister sent by the governess. Because of his intervention, Moll's death sentence was commuted to transportation to the American colonies. While in prison Moll re-encountered Jemmy, a highwayman who was her most recent living husband. She persuaded him to join her on the ship transporting convicts to the colonies. This they accomplished and settled in Maryland, where they became successful plantation-owners in about a year's time.

In Virginia, Moll's former husband-brother was living with one of their sons. Moll was anxious to receive her inheritance from her mother's estate and to meet her son, but was equally reluctant to confront her brother. Everything turned out all right for Moll: she was able to get her inheritance, she was able to avoid her brother, and she met her son, who proved to be devoted and fair.

At the age of almost seventy, Moll returned with Jemmy to London, where they planned to live out their lives in repentance for their criminal activities.

NOTE: The original of *Moll Flanders* does not have chapter divisions. To provide greater clarity in the summaries and discussions, we have divided the novel into chapters.

CHAPTER SUMMARIES
AND DISCUSSIONS

CHAPTER 1

SYNOPSIS: Early Life

My true name is so well known in the records or registers at Newgate, and in the Old Bailey, and there are some things of such consequence still depending there, relating to my particular conduct, that it is not to be expected I should set my name or the account of my family to this work; perhaps, after my death, it may be better known; at present it would not be proper, no, not though a general pardon should be issued, even without exceptions and reserve of persons or crimes.

Moll Flanders, as our character is called by her criminal associates, was born in Newgate Prison in London, England, where her mother was imprisoned for a petty theft. Moll tells us, in this personal history of her life, that after her birth, her mother was "transported to the plantations." Moll believes that she herself fell into bad hands and, until she was three years old, lived with gypsies from whom she then fled.

Because she was too young to work, the town authorities put Moll in the charge of a well-bred but poor woman whom Moll called "nurse." This woman kept a small school where Moll was taught reading, needlework, and manners.

At the age of eight Moll became terrified by the news that the town authorities planned to make her a household servant. She begged her nurse to allow her to remain with her and sew for her living. Her appeal was so forceful and constant that the nurse resolved to ask the Mayor to allow Moll to stay with her until she was older. This concession did not satisfy Moll, who was determined to become a "gentlewoman" when she grew up and to make her living in a business of her own. Her strong determination not to become a household servant amused the nurse, the Mayor, his wife, and their two daughters, since Moll's idea of a gentlewoman was quite different from the idea held by the others. Moll understood the term to designate a woman who was successfully self-employed, whereas the others meant one who lived well, rich, and high. The kind of woman Moll had in mind was a neighbor who appeared to make her living by her needlework. Her nurse explained that the woman was, in fact, a prostitute; but Moll, not understanding this explanation, resolutely insisted that the woman was a gentlewoman who did not go into service or do housework, and that she would be such a gentlewoman as that. This further amused the Mayor's wife and daughters, who frequently visited Moll to see her needlework and give her money for living expenses. Her manners and conversation were so appealing that Moll soon became a favorite of the prosperous matrons of the town, who also brought her sewing to do.

When Moll was about ten years old, she again feared the town authorities might send her into service. Fortunately, by this time Moll was earning enough money from her needlework to maintain herself. Therefore, her nurse requested Moll's services as her assistant. In addition, Moll endeared herself to the rich matrons so that they gave her clothes and money more often than formerly. At twelve, Moll could buy her own clothes and pay for her keep.

When she was thirteen, Moll was invited to live for a week with one of the matrons and her two daughters. About a year later, Moll's nurse died, leaving Moll to face the world alone. Soon, however, the lady in whose family Moll had spent a week sent for her to come and live with her family. The Mayoress and other prosperous matrons were all a little angry, because they had hoped to have Moll live with them.

DISCUSSION

Moll Flanders was given this name by her criminal associates; she used it throughout this autobiographical account so as not to cause her family any embarrassment or to expose herself to any danger from some previous vicious criminal acquaintances now that she had repented for her crimes.

Newgate Prison, Moll's birthplace, became a shadow over her entire life.

At this time in history, England sent many of her prisoners

(Moll's mother, for instance) to her colony, America, when her prisons became too full to hold them all. These criminals became convict laborers, and some worked out their time on the plantations of Virginia and Maryland. After serving their time, many later became plantation-owners themselves.

At the beginning of the novel, Moll explains how some other countries provide for orphans by assigning them to a hospital called the House of Orphans where they are cared for and taught a trade until they are able to provide for themselves. In the first chapter Moll points up England's irresponsibility toward her orphans. This is a foreshadowing of Moll's development into a thief and prostitute.

Moll's "nurse" was her foster mother. The term applies to women whom the magistrates or town authorities made guardians of orphans until they were old enough to become servants in the homes of the rich.

The desire to become a gentlewoman rather than a servant is the motivating theme of Moll's life. Here we see Moll as a determined and independent character who refused to change her goal in life despite the means she had to employ. Moll determined to become self-employed and resist being sent into service.

QUESTION

Describe the kind of problems Moll might have because she is an orphan. Does an orphan of today have the same problems? Why or why not?

CHAPTER 2

SYNOPSIS: Girlhood

Moll lived with this respectable family until she was almost eighteen years old. Just by being around the daughters during their lessons, Moll learned how to dance, to speak French, to write, and to sing. In fact, she outshone the daughters in everything becoming to a gentlewoman—including beauty—in every respect save one; she had no fortune. Moll was vain about her beauty and was impressed by anyone who commented upon it. Nevertheless, she "had the character too of a very sober, modest, and virtuous young woman," who as yet did not know "what a temptation to wickedness meant."

Soon her great beauty was noticed by both sons of the family and frequently commented upon by them. The elder son was a good-looking, smooth-talking, young man who plotted to seduce Mrs. Betty, as Moll was called. Robin, the younger son, was also attracted to Moll. The family, however, did not worry about the attentions paid to Moll by the sons, for Moll had no fortune.

As fate would have it, the elder son persistently contrived to be alone with the innocent Moll; he bestowed kisses on her lips and guineas (gold coins) in her hands, while declaring his love for her. Since this was Moll's first love affair, she became overwhelmed by the attentions of the elder son and weakened with each encounter. His warmth destroyed her loneliness and his gold erased her poverty. As Moll explains, her vanity was her downfall. She warns young girls to beware of being vain about their beauty, for this vanity causes a young girl not to doubt any man who says he is in love with her.

As time passed, the elder son, persistent in his pursuit, showered Moll with money. Meanwhile, Moll fell deeper and deeper in love. In order to deceive the family about the true state of affairs, Moll treated the elder son quite coolly in the presence of his family.

One afternoon the elder brother slipped a note to Mrs. Betty (Moll) instructing her that he would send her on an errand the next day and then meet her on the way. The next morning, loudly instructing her to go on several errands for him, he told his family he was going to visit a gentleman and asked his sisters to go with him. They refused because they were expecting some company—as he well knew. Just then Sir W............. H.............'s coach drove up. The elder brother announced that Sir W............. desired to speak to him on some urgent business so he dashed off in the coach, only to pick up Mrs. Betty (Moll) as she made her way to the stores on his errands. All, of course, was pre-arranged and the two were driven to the home of a confidant of his where everything was convenient for mischief and wickedness.

The elder brother declared his love for Moll. He promised to provide for her if she should become pregnant and to marry her as soon as he came into his inheritance. Thus Moll accepted his gift of one hundred guineas, and his promise to give her the same amount each year until they were married. After this Moll made no more resistance to him. Later she performed the errands he had instructed her to, then hurried home. The elder brother stayed out until late at night so there would be no suspicion in the family.

DISCUSSION

Notice that in spite of Moll's declarations about not going into service, she was in fact a servant in this home. Nevertheless, she was treated more as a friend than as a servant.

Moll's vanity was her downfall. Since she believed herself to be beautiful, it was not difficult for her to believe that her beauty could cause even a rich young man to fall in love with her. Therefore, she sincerely believed the elder brother's professions of love and promises to marry her when he came into his inheritance. His compliments and gifts caused her to give up her virtue too easily.

Guineas are gold coins that were used in England during the seventeenth century.

QUESTION

Do you think the elder son would have married Moll if he had not succeeded in seducing her? Explain your answer.

CHAPTER 3

SYNOPSIS: Marriage of Convenience

Six months after the affair with the elder brother had begun, Moll received a proposal of marriage from Robin, the younger brother. Believing that the elder brother truly intended to marry her, she resisted Robin's proposal by presenting such arguments against it as her lowly status and the family's probable disapproval of the match. Because Robin was honest and innocent, he often talked about Mrs. Betty to his sisters. Soon they began to suspect that he loved her and became cool toward Moll. She was distressed by the family's changed behavior toward her, but she was more distressed by the realization that she had been the elder brother's mistress when she could have been the younger brother's wife.

Soon Moll decided to tell the elder brother that Robin loved her. In telling the story Moll led the elder brother to believe that the family thought she and he were having an affair. Laughingly, the elder brother told Moll that the family suspected Robin, not him, of having an affair with her.

Seeing she was getting nowhere with the elder brother, Moll told him of Robin's proposal of marriage. The elder brother was surprised by this and sought time to consider it. Meanwhile, he cautioned her neither to consent nor to give Robin a flat denial. This, of course, startled Moll, who reminded the elder brother that she had no consent to give Robin since she was engaged to him. The elder brother pacified Moll as best he could.

As soon as possible he confronted Robin with the family's suspicions. Robin admitted he loved Moll deeply and intended to marry her. Some time later the elder brother repeated the entire conversation to Moll and sought to persuade her to marry Robin, saying that the family would become suspicious of her turning down such a good catch without another in sight. This shocked Moll greatly, for she still believed the elder brother loved her and would be faithful to his promise to marry her. The elder brother denied having broken any of his promises to her, saying that he had promised to marry her when he came into his estate but that his father was a hale and healthy man who might live thirty years longer. He promised never to reveal the secret of their affair and to treat Moll with great respect when she and Robin were married.

Because she "loved to distraction" the older brother, Moll was very much upset by this decision and was quite ill for several weeks. The family fell into arguments over Moll, the sisters complaining about her vanity, the mother worried about Moll's involvement with Robin. Meanwhile, the elder brother contrived to bring about a marriage between Moll and Robin in order to relieve himself of his involvement in the affair.

Robin by his sincerity finally persuaded his mother to accept the match. The family was also impressed by Moll's obvious reluctance to marry Robin; they reasoned that her reluctance proved she was not a fortune-hunter. The elder brother convinced Moll she should marry Robin or face the prospect of being left alone in the world to shift for herself.

DISCUSSION

In eighteenth-century England people were very much conscious of social position. Marriages between the wealthy and the poor were infrequent. For this reason "marriages of convenience" were often arranged. In a marriage of convenience each person sought to improve his position in some way. For example, a young man with a title and no money might marry a young lady with money and no title. Therefore, the elder brother's attitude toward marriage was typical for the times, while Robin's attitude was rather unusual since Moll had neither money nor social position.

The elder son was attracted to Moll's beauty, but he did not love her. He wanted her as a mistress but not as a wife. On the other hand, Robin actually loved Moll.

The elder son would have disgraced his family if he had married a girl without money or social position. Since he did not want to ruin his chances of collecting his inheritance after his father's death, he was determined not to have any scandal attached to his name. Therefore, to rid himself of his involvement with Moll, he thrust her into a marriage with his brother.

QUESTION

What kind of life do you think Moll will have with Robin, since she does not love him?

CHAPTER 4

SYNOPSIS: The Young Widow

Although Moll "had not the least affection" for Robin, the two were married and lived together for five years, at the end of which time he died. During their marriage he was very good to her, and they lived together contentedly. Since Robin received little money from his family, he was able to leave but little money after his death. Nevertheless, with the £500 which Moll had received from the elder brother as a bribe for her to marry Robin, other money which he had previously given her and which she had saved, and the amount which her husband had left, Moll began her widowhood with about £1200. The two children which resulted from the marriage were taken off her hands by Robin's mother and father. At the age of about twenty-four, the beautiful Moll was left alone again, to make her way in the world.

Moll was not too much saddened by the loss of her husband because she did not really love him. The brother she did love was often around while they lived in the country. Her feelings for Robin's brother were so strong that, she said, "I never was in bed with my husband but I wished myself in the arms of his brother." When they were invited to attend the elder brother's wedding, she had pretended to be ill so that she would not have to go.

Moll's intention now was to marry well. She took a room in the home of a linen-draper, whose sister was an acquaintance of Moll's. The linen-draper began to court Moll, who continued to meet other admirers through her landlord's sister, a gay, wild woman who brought callers around to meet the pretty young widow. None of those she liked proposed marriage, and those who did propose were the dullest of the lot. Most of those who courted her were tradesmen, whom Moll did not mind as long as they could act the part of a nobleman.

Finally, she found a "gentleman-tradesman," a man of style, who was a draper. She had spurned her landlord, also a draper, because it appeared he preferred a mistress to a wife. She married the gentleman-tradesman only to discover that he was a "rake, gentleman, shopkeeper, and beggar" all rolled into one. For three months he enjoyed Moll, using her money for such things as a long vacation in the country. Although most of Moll's money soon was gone, her husband continued to make debts freely. Because of his extravagant tastes Moll's husband was completely broke at the end of somewhat more than two years of marriage. Foreseeing this possibility, however, Moll had saved some of her money for herself.

Eventually her husband was arrested for debt and put in "a sponging-house" (a place of confinement for debtors). He sent for Moll and told her to go home and in the night to take away all of her valuables so that the creditors could not get them.

Next he told her to go to his shop and, if possible, take £100 or £200 in goods. Also, he told her of his plan to escape to France.

Moll did as her husband instructed her. Later, she learned that he had escaped and gone to France. From there, he sent information about where he had pawned goods worth about £120. Moll redeemed the goods and resold them for a profit of about £100.

Now Moll was troubled. As she said, "I had a husband and no husband." She felt she was unable to remarry although she knew her husband would not return. With only about £500, distressed and friendless, Moll changed her name and her rooms in order to avoid her husband's creditors. She went into a section of town called the Mint, took rooms in an out-of-the-way place, dressed herself as a widow, and changed her name to "Mrs. Flanders."

DISCUSSION

Moll's vanity again caused her distress. It led her, first, to marry a rogue because of his pretty words and ways; and second, to become a dodger from the law because she had followed her husband's instructions to take goods from his shop and hide them from his creditors.

The Mint is a slum area of London, housing the poor and the criminal element of the town.

The expression "to wear the mark of his trade upon him" means that in the evening a shopkeeper looked as though he still had his apron on or a tradesman still had the ring of his cap on his forehead which would emphasize that they were not real gentlemen but rather what they were: shopkeepers or tradesmen.

QUESTION

What about Moll is revealed in her ready relinquishment of her two children to their grandparents?

CHAPTER 5

SYNOPSIS: The Fugitive Widow

Even though Moll was hiding in the Mint among "the

sons of affliction," she continued to have many admirers. She discovered that the men in the Mint, though poor, always seemed to have money for drinking and carousing. But she decided they were too wicked even for her. With plenty of time to think, Moll reflected upon her present condition and the course her life would now have to take. She had no friends or relatives and little money left. Because she felt disgusted with the people in the Mint and with the way she had lived previously, she decided to leave.

While Moll was living in the Mint, she had become friendly with a widow whose husband had been captain of a merchant ship. This widow, too, had taken refuge in the Mint in an attempt to escape her creditors. However, with the help of friends she was able to pay them off and was free to return to her home in another part of town.

After discovering that Moll was not a criminal, the widow invited Moll to live with her, suggesting that one of the ship captains might like her. Hoping to find a husband, Moll had accepted the invitation. But six months later, the widow found one, instead.

Most of Moll's money had been spent by this time. Most of her suitors, too, were looking for a woman with money or influential friends. Moll discovered that in London one married for money and position, not love. Men openly went fortune-hunting, although they themselves had no fortunes, and rejected women who even inquired about their character or finances. Moll had this clearly demonstrated to her because of what happened to a friend of hers, a woman who attempted to find out something about her suitor's background and who was consequently rejected by the suitor.

Moll convinced this friend that she should resent being rejected thus and that she should seek revenge by ruining his reputation. Moll said that if the woman did not avenge herself, she would be held in contempt by the other women in that part of town. After listening to Moll very carefully, the friend agreed that she would like either to have her suitor back or to ruin his reputation. Moll planned a campaign to get him back. They decided to smear his name by spreading rumors that he was penniless, bad-tempered, and bigamous. The campaign worked so well that no other woman in that part of town allowed him to court her. Soon he was frantic to see Moll's friend; when she finally allowed him to call on her, she confronted him with the various stories which the two women had invented. Because he was now eager to marry her, the man, a captain, brought proof that he had paid for his part of the ship and proof from the owners that they had no intention of removing him from the command of the ship. Therefore, Moll's friend decided she would marry the seaman, since he now was quite humble enough. And so they were married, the seaman still ignorant of the amount of his wife's fortune. Thus the young lady made the seaman feel that obtaining her was the most difficult thing in the world and, in a sense, turned the tables on him. In addition, she put part of her fortune in trust, without letting him know anything of it; the rest she gave to him after a time, and thus assured his good treatment of her.

DISCUSSION

Moll felt that men got the best of the deal in courtship and marriage. A woman was supposed to feel that a man had done her a favor by asking her to marry him. If she turned him down, she was not asked again. And if he was refused at one house, he would be received at another. In addition, a woman was supposed to be content to remain ignorant of her suitor's background. This situation distressed Moll, and she was determined to change it.

Because the seaman was so arrogant, Moll and her acquaintance were able to humble him by destroying his reputation among the other women in town.

The saying,

> A woman's ne'er so ruined but she can
> Revenge herself on her undoer, Man,

means that a woman's reputation is never so completely ruined that she cannot ruin a man's as well.

In this chapter Moll began moralizing about life when she said that men have so much choice among women. She further said that women who cheapen themselves by being too easy to get are not worth having.

QUESTION

Why is Moll so concerned about the outcome of her friend's affair with the seaman?

CHAPTER 6

SYNOPSIS: Match-making

Since Moll had learned from this match-making venture that a woman should put a value on herself, she determined to move to a place where no one knew that she was a widow without money. She confided in her friend, the captain's lady, disclosing her near-penniless condition. The captain's lady was as good a friend to Moll as Moll had been to her, and from time to time gave Moll money for her maintenance so she wouldn't have to spend her few remaining pounds. Furthermore, the captain's lady suggested that if Moll would put herself entirely in her hands, she would help her get a rich husband. This Moll did; through deceit and conniving, the captain's lady led her husband to believe that Moll had a fortune of at least £1500 and might inherit more. He, in turn, conveyed this information around the neighborhood. This plan worked and Moll was able to select her prospective husband from among many suitors. The man she chose she selected on the basis of his avowals of great love for her. Though Moll often accused him of wanting to marry her for her money, her admirer assured her that this was not true and laughed at her jokes about her poverty. By telling her admirer that she cared not to know about his fortune, she learned that he had three plantations in Virginia and a comfortable income as well. When Moll said she did not care to live in Virginia, he assured her that they would not go if she did not wish to do so.

DISCUSSION

Both Moll and the captain's lady proved increasingly adept at deceiving men. Since Moll had already been deceived by two men—the elder brother and the draper—perhaps she honestly felt that this was the only way for a woman to manage. It is important to note, however, that Moll truly liked and respected her suitor and thought "how doubly criminal it was to deceive such a man."

Moll's suitor's estate was valued at £1200 a year if he lived on it and £300 a year if he did not.

QUESTION

Moll has persisted in telling her suitor that she is poor.

What do you think his attitude will be toward Moll when he learns she is telling the truth?

CHAPTER 7

SYNOPSIS: Happiness

Moll married again. After a fortnight she told her husband it was time for him to know how much money she had brought to their marriage. He declared it did not matter, since he had got the woman he loved. Nevertheless, Moll insisted on telling her husband that she understood the captain had told him that she had a great deal more money than she actually had and that she had never asked the captain to do so. Her husband insisted it did not matter if she had less than he was told, since Moll had not deceived him. At this, Moll gave him £160. Her husband seemed not too distressed, as Moll had cleverly led him to believe she had nothing at all. Later she brought him £100 more. After about a week, she brought him £180 more and about £60 in linen and led him to believe she had paid a debt with the rest. When she told her husband she had no more money at all, he seemed grateful for what she had given him. Nevertheless, because he had expected more money from Moll and because he was receiving less in income from his plantations than he had counted on, Moll's husband began talking about taking her to Virginia. Moll agreed that this was the best course of action under the circumstances. He told Moll that he had "a very good house" in Virginia and that his mother, his only relative beside a sister, lived there.

After a long and dangerous voyage, during which most of their possessions were stolen by pirates, they arrived in Virginia, where they went to their plantation. They were affectionately received by his mother and all three lived together on the plantation.

DISCUSSION

Notice how Moll led her husband to believe she had no money at all so that he would not be too disappointed when she gave him the little she did have. In this chapter she warned women that this could be a dangerous step, for it could lead to abuse later on.

QUESTION

How would you weigh Moll's frankness against her deceit? Be explicit in illustrating your answer.

CHAPTER 8

SYNOPSIS: A Tragic Marriage

Moll was very happy until her mother-in-law, a good-humored old woman, began one of the numerous stories of her youth. She told Moll that most of the inhabitants of the colony had either been brought by captains of ships and sold as servants or "transported from Newgate and other prisons, after having been found guilty of felony and other crimes punishable with death." They worked out their time and then were given a few acres of land by the government, were encouraged to work the land, and were extended credit for tools and other necessities by local tradesmen and merchants. Many, she told Moll, became great men and were not ashamed of the brand on their hands which indicated that they had been in prison. Then she took off her glove and showed Moll the burn in her own hand. Moll's mother-in-law related that she had fallen into bad company in her youth and was saved from hanging only because she was pregnant. When the mother-in-law happened to mention her own name, Moll became very much upset and begged her mother-in-law to discontinue her story. Nevertheless, the woman went on to say that she had eventually married her master, after the death of his wife, and had brought up the two children she had had by him. At this point, Moll felt certain that her mother-in-law was her own mother, and that the two children she herself had, and the third on the way, were all got by her own brother. Moll was horrified by this knowledge but decided to keep it to herself, sure that she would be even further "undone" if either her mother or her brother learned the truth.

Moll was now a most unhappy woman and lived for three more years "with the greatest pressure imaginable"; but she had no more children. Her mother continued telling her of her past life of prostitution, thievery, and prison. Soon Moll's anguish became noticeable and caused her husband to be jealous and act unkindly toward her. Taking him up on an earlier promise, Moll begged her husband to allow her to return to England, saying only that Virginia was not agreeable to her. Her brother—as she now viewed her husband—refused her appeal. They quarreled frequently and heatedly; he called her "an unnatural mother" for being willing to leave her children; she refused to sleep with him any more. Moll's behavior was so inexplicable to her brother that he threatened to put her "into a madhouse." Thoroughly frightened by this threat and distressed by the whole situation, Moll determined to tell the truth to someone. But before she could decide how and to whom to speak, she had a particularly fierce quarrel with her brother and was provoked into telling him that he was not her lawful husband nor were their childen legal. Her half-confession caused him to become quite ill. He begged her to explain her words, but she refused. Finding Moll adamant on this point, he finally told his mother about their trouble and urged her to get the secret from Moll. Eventually, Moll told her mother-in-law that she believed she was her long-lost daughter. She made her promise to keep this information secret unless Moll gave her permission to reveal it. When she recovered from her astonishment, Moll's mother-in-law, now her acknowledged mother, advised Moll to "bury the whole thing entirely" and try to restore harmony within the family. Finding this advice distasteful, Moll asked her mother to convince her son that Moll should be allowed to return to England. Although the two women could not reconcile their differences, a kind of truce was established between Moll and her brother. In this easier atmosphere, Moll found it possible to tell her brother their true relationship. Understandably shocked, he first fell ill, then unsuccessfully attempted suicide. Finally, however, they agreed that she would return to England; that he would pretend she was dead; that they would continue to correspond, as brother and sister; and that he would support her as long as she lived. Accordingly, Moll sailed for England in August, having lived in America for eight years.

DISCUSSION

Moll's behavior in this chapter shows both her strong

determination to look out for herself and her real concern for her husband/brother, whom she honestly liked. Note the different reactions to Moll's secret. Note, too, that Moll again found it necessary to leave her children.

QUESTIONS

How are Moll and her mother alike? How do they differ?

CHAPTER 9

SYNOPSIS: A Return to London

After a stormy journey, Moll finally arrived in London with a good part of her possessions spoiled and only about £300 with which to begin a new life. She was without friends, for she found it unwise to renew old acquaintances, and the captain and his lady who had helped Moll to get married were dead.

Moll went to Bristol to reclaim her lost cargo and from there to Bath, where she hoped that something would happen to improve her situation. There she met some bad acquaintances and some gay company but had to spend a good part of her money in the process of seeking another husband. She soon discovered that Bath was a place where men sought mistresses but not wives. While in Bath, though, she did become friendly with a woman of bad reputation, in whose house she lived. She remained for a year in Bath, for she discovered it was cheaper there than anywhere else. Sometimes, however, she felt sad and alone, especially during the winter.

When Moll revealed her circumstances—the loss of her possessions but the expectation of financial help from Virginia—to her landlady, she was very sympathetic. In the spring a gentleman who had earlier singled out Moll for his attentions came to lodge in the same house as Moll. He was a married man but his wife "was distempered in her head." The landlady encouraged Moll to take money for keeping him company, but Moll refused. The landlady then manipulated the situation so that the gentleman inquired into Moll's circumstances without any prompting from Moll. For several weeks Moll withstood his repeated suggestions that he help her financially. Then Moll's landlady took matters into her own hands and deceived the gentleman in Moll's presence by saying that the money Moll was supposed to receive from Virginia had not come. Although Moll rather angrily answered that she had all the money she needed, her admirer insisted that she show him just how much she had. Upon seeing her small store of coins, he thrust more money on her, saying it was a gift not a loan. In return for this kindness, Moll cooked and served his meals.

DISCUSSION

Bath is a fashionable spa in Somerset, England.

Notice that Moll makes a point of mentioning that she was still far from being old.

QUESTION

Why do you think Moll resists her landlady's repeated suggestions that she take money from the gentleman she met at Bath?

CHAPTER 10

SYNOPSIS: Another Lover

Three months later, when the season ended at Bath, the gentleman invited Moll to accompany him to London. Before she had decided whether or not to do so, he became quite ill on a business trip, and sent for Moll. She brought him back to Bath and nursed him through his illness. After this, they became quite close, though not lovers, and remained so for two years. One night, however, after drinking too much wine, Moll suggested they make love. Though penitent, they continued this close relationship until Moll became pregnant.

When Moll told her lover and her landlady about her condition, the landlady made arrangements for Moll to meet a midwife and a nurse. Meanwhile, the landlady deceived the town authorities with a tale that Moll was the wife of a wealthy lord. The authorities were satisfied with the story, and Moll was given excellent—and expensive—care when she "was brought to bed of a fine boy." Then Moll's gentleman friend sent for her to come to London where he had provided an apartment for her.

Moll lived six years in this happy state, but then her lover became ill; since some of his wife's relatives were with him, Moll could not go to him. She wrote several letters to her lover, but receiving no answer, she disguised herself as a servant and visited his home. While there she gossiped with a maid who told her the master was very ill and not expected to live. After about two weeks of anxious waiting, Moll learned that his health was improving. She waited four more months to hear from him, but no word came. Finally, she wrote a note reminding her lover of his responsibility to her and their child. She received a formal reply which said their affair was over and suggested she use the enclosed £50 to pay her rent and her travel expenses to Bath. He promised to "take due care of the child" but insisted that he and Moll never see each other again. Greatly upset by the letter, Moll decided that his close brush with death had caused her lover to so much regret his involvement with her that he now hated her.

She sent him another note, saying that she did not plan to return to Bath and promised that if he sent her another £50 she would sign a paper releasing him completely from his obligations to her. She decided to leave her son where he was and told her former lover that she intended to go back to Virginia where, if all turned out well, she would later summon her son. Moll acknowledges that she had no intention of returning to Virginia but thought that the lie would be more convincing. Her note worked, in any case, and she received another £50.

Moll reviewed her position and discovered that her situation was not so bad. She had some goods from her brother, about £130, and a good wardrobe with which to begin a new life. She realized, though, that she was now forty-two years old, which was quite different from twenty-five.

DISCUSSION

Notice that Moll seemed to like married life. Her account showed no instances where she went astray while her husbands lived.

Note also that Moll had quite extraordinarily bad luck with her husbands or lovers. Some died, one left her, one she left for a good reason, and one left the country to avoid arrest.

QUESTION

In view of her past life, what sort of pattern do you think Moll's future life will follow?

CHAPTER 11

SYNOPSIS: Another Courtship

Moll was alone again without adviser or friend; unable to advise herself, she lost one hundred pounds which she had entrusted to a goldsmith. Knowing that she wanted a settled life but not how to obtain it, she lived frugally on her small store of money. All she wanted was to find "a sober, good husband," and she reminisced that she had given her husbands no trouble on account of her behavior.

Soon, in the house where she lodged, Moll met a north-country woman, thought to be a gentlewoman, who often spoke of the cheapness of living in the country. This woman, believing that she had quite a substantial fortune, invited Moll to visit her in Lancashire. She also told Moll that she had a brother who was "a considerable gentleman." Before accepting the woman's invitation, Moll wanted to put what money she had in a safe place: she didn't want to carry it around with her.

Moll was in great distress because she knew no one in London she could trust to care for her possessions and money. One morning, however, it occurred to Moll to seek help at the bank where she often had gone to receive interest from her savings. There she found a sympathetic clerk who directed her to a friend of his, another bank clerk, who handled cases such as Moll's during his spare time. Impressed by his "sincere disinterested honesty," Moll asked him to handle her financial affairs.

Moll had occasion to meet several times with this bank clerk, and during the course of their conversations she discovered that he was lonely because his wife had left him for another man. Finding Moll a charming and agreeable woman, he asked her advice about what he should do about his wife. On Moll's suggestion that he get a divorce, he proposed that he and Moll marry as soon as he was free. Moll was delighted by the proposal but refused to give him a definite answer. The next evening, while Moll was dining with the clerk, he suggested, first, that Moll "marry" him while they waited for the divorce; on her refusal of this suggestion, he next asked that she sign a contract of agreement to marry him as soon as he won a divorce from his wife. Although tempted, Moll declined to do this; she was thinking of the lady who had invited her to go to Lancashire and who had seemed to promise great fortunes. Therefore, Moll told her clerk that she was going into the north and that he could correspond with her there. She was careful, though, to leave the impression that she would marry him on her return.

Moll went with her acquaintance into Lancashire; on the way the woman's brother met the two ladies in a coach and carried them in great style to Liverpool, where they were handsomely entertained by a merchant. From there they went to the home of an uncle. For six months Moll was seriously courted by her friend's brother, who had been led to believe that Moll had £15,000; in turn, he was said to have a fortune of at least £1500 a year, most of it in Ireland. After an expensive courtship, and his promise to buy, in partnership with Moll, land worth £600 a year, Moll consented to be married in a private ceremony. Giving only a few thoughts to her bank clerk in London, Moll admitted to being dazzled by thoughts of money, expensive presents, a large estate, and other fine things.

DISCUSSION

Although Moll seemed able to recognize the bank clerk as an honest man, she was less perceptive about the "friend" and the friend's "brother." Both Moll and her suitor act as though a really frank discussion of money would be beneath them; therefore, they are both in for an unpleasant discovery.

QUESTION

Why did Moll leave the bank clerk, an almost-certain prospect, to go to the country?

CHAPTER 12

SYNOPSIS: Another Marriage

After about two months of happy marriage and expensive living, Moll's husband suggested they go to his estate in Ireland. He also suggested that Moll would probably want to return to London to settle her affairs and to transfer her funds to Ireland. Moll, startled at this suggestion, said she had no affairs to settle. Thus began the revelation of truth: Moll discovered that her "friend" had deceived both Moll and her husband by telling her "brother" that Moll had a great fortune, and by telling Moll that the gentleman was her brother when actually he was an ex-lover. Moll also discovered that there was no estate in Ireland and that, obviously, her husband had no intention of going there. However, both realized their affection for each other and regretted that they could not remain together since neither had much money.

When Moll awoke one morning she discovered that Jemmy, her husband, had gone, leaving her a broken heart, a note, two guineas, his gold watch, and two little rings, one diamond and one gold. Having spent the day grieving his departure, Moll was surprised and delighted when Jemmy returned at nightfall, saying he could not bear to be away from her. He said he would accompany her to the outskirts of London, but would not discuss why he would go no further. Moll persuaded him to stay with her for a while in an inn about thirty miles outside London, while she tried to think of a way for them to stay together. She told Jemmy about the plantation in Virginia and tried to convince him that they could quite easily make a good living there. However, he rejected this plan and suggested that he go to Ireland to try to make his fortune; if he failed, they then might consider going to Virginia. After a month the two parted, with directions about how to get in touch with each other.

DISCUSSION

The focal point of this chapter is the deep affection between Jemmy and Moll. Even though Jemmy left, he returned because he could not bear to be parted from Moll.

QUESTION

Moll told each of her husbands that she had not deceived him about her lack of money. How would you interpret her allowing other women to spread rumors about her wealth?

CHAPTER 13

SYNOPSIS: Another Child

Moll moved into London the day after Jemmy left. There she reflected happily on the pleasant hours she had spent with him; this happiness was short-lived, however, because she discovered she was pregnant. The one bright light was that, through her correspondence with the bank clerk during these seven months, she knew he was having trouble obtaining his divorce. This was welcome news since Moll was now in no position to resume their relationship.

Moll's problem now consisted of her pregnancy, her friendlessness, and her despondency. Together, these problems made her very ill, and made her think she might have a miscarriage. She says that, although she would not have induced a miscarriage, she would not have minded if she had miscarried naturally.

Luckily, Moll's landlady arranged for Moll to meet a midwife who had a business of caring for pregnant women, particularly unwed ones. Now that Moll's most immediate problem was taken care of, she began to feel much better. The midwife invited her to come to her house, offering her a choice of three variously priced forms of service. When Moll apologetically selected the cheapest rate, the midwife explained there was no need for apology, since many of her customers paid the higher rates, thus balancing out the expenses.

When Moll moved into the midwife's house, where she was treated with great courtesy and care, she was shocked to learn that most of the midwife's patients were prostitutes.

While Moll was at the midwife's, she received a letter from her banker friend, saying that he was nearing the end of his divorce suit and that he still wanted Moll to marry him. Moll sent a reply to the banker by way of Liverpool, wishing him well but not answering his proposal.

Moll had her baby, a boy, about the middle of May; a few weeks later she received another letter from the banker, saying the divorce was final and his wife had committed suicide. He begged Moll to see him so that they could further discuss their relationship. This so complicated life for Moll that she told the midwife about the problem of trying to keep the child under the circumstances. After much talk, the midwife convinced Moll to give up her child for adoption. This Moll agreed to do, if she could see the child from time to time.

DISCUSSION

At this point, it might help to summarize Moll's marital

history to date: she had been married four times and was now contemplating a fifth marriage. Her husbands thus far were Robin, who died; the draper, who left the country because of his debts; her brother, whom she left in Virginia; and Jemmy, whom she dearly loved. Her new prospect was a banker who had just succeeded in obtaining a divorce from his wife. Moll has never divorced anyone.

A midwife is a woman who assists women in childbirth. In no instance yet had Moll had a doctor to deliver her babies. This is evidence of the fact that doctors were scarce in England during the seventeenth century. Therefore, it was the custom for some women to practice midwifery.

Notice the close tie between Moll and the midwife. These two are to meet again.

Notice, too, how Moll sent her letters to the banker by circuitous routes. In this way Moll was able to remain in London while leading the banker to believe she was elsewhere.

QUESTION

Why is Moll so cautious about letting the banker know her exact whereabouts?

CHAPTER 14

SYNOPSIS: A Surprising Event

Moll now began to correspond regularly with her friend at the bank. About the beginning of July she wrote him that she planned to be in town in August. The banker said he would arrange to meet her. Because she wanted the banker to believe that she had been in the country all of this time, Moll arranged her trip in such a way as to deceive him about her true whereabouts. When they did meet, the banker insisted on Moll's staying at an inn to rest up from her journey. While they were in the inn, the banker persuaded Moll to marry him. She reproached herself for her past life but, nevertheless, decided to marry the banker. After further eager persuasion by the banker, they were married that evening in the inn.

The next day as Moll was looking out the window, she saw Jemmy, her Lancashire husband, drive up to an inn next to the one Moll was staying at. He and two companions went in and took a room. All this thoroughly frightened Moll, for she feared Jemmy might see her. Before this could happen, though, Jemmy and his companions rode off in a great hurry. That night there was a great uproar in the street, as several men came riding by in pursuit of three highwaymen. The inn where Jemmy and his two companions had stayed was searched. In order to throw the chasers off the track, Moll said she knew one of the men to be a very honest person with a large estate in Lancashire. She also told this story to the policeman, explaining that she had seen the three gentlemen when they arrived, when they were at their dinner, and later when they left the inn. She explained that she could make the identification since she herself had just left Lancashire.

This information stopped the mob and the police. Moll did not know exactly what had happened, but she did hear that some coaches had been robbed at Dunstable Hill.

Moll and her husband remained at the inn four more days in spite of his insistence that it was safest to travel right after a robbery, for the thieves would have fled to evade pursuers. Moll resisted leaving immediately for fear she would chance to see her old husband on the road. She was quite happy about her husband's treatment of her, although her remorse about her past life recurred periodically.

On the fifth day, they left the inn with their landlord, his son, and three armed companions who guarded their coach into Dunstable.

Because Moll was now married, she had no worries about where to stay in London, where she now knew no one. It was possible for her to go directly to her new husband's home with him and take possession at once of a well-furnished house and a man with money.

Now Moll was very happy about her anticipated life with the banker. She reflected on her past life and felt repentance for the things she had done. She remembered her lover at Bath who had abandoned her in spite of his love, and how from fear of poverty she had resorted to using her beauty to get what she wanted, a secure existence. In her own words, "Now I seemed landed in a safe harbour, after the stormy voyage of life past was at an end, and I began to be thankful for my deliverance." She spent many hours weeping over her past follies and her wicked life, and sometimes flattered herself that she had really repented. But she wound up condoning her actions, saying that her fear of poverty was so great that it weakened her ability to resist the temptation to sin.

DISCUSSION

Moll expressed remorse in this chapter about the trick she was about to play on the banker, a kind good man who had just divorced a whore and was about to marry her, who was not much better. She called attention to the fact that her mother had been a whore and a thief, Moll herself had been born in Newgate Prison, had lain with two brothers, had had three children by her own brother, had slept with thirteen men, and had married and had a child since she met her present husband. After reproaching herself for a time, she resolved to be true to the banker and make him a good wife.

Notice how Moll played hard to get in order to make herself a more desirable catch.

All of Moll's marriages have been very private affairs. Why is she so concerned about keeping her affairs private? Remember the move to the Mint, the name-change to Mrs. Flanders, the seclusion during her pregnancies, as well as the secret marriages. In this chapter Moll contrasted a life of virtue and sobriety with one of looseness, extravagance, and wickedness. What excuse does she offer for the need to live a life of wickedness and evil?

QUESTION

What hints of future trouble are given in this chapter?

CHAPTER 15

SYNOPSIS: The Turning Point

Life was now tranquil, for the banker husband was quiet, sensible, and virtuous. In business he was hard-working and just and was able to provide his family with a good living. Moll chose to live a retired and frugal life, and, therefore, they did not visit or have visitors. For five years their life was one of contentment and ease.

Then, however, the banker trusted a fellow-clerk with a large sum of money, which he lost; although the loss was great, the disaster need not have been too much for Moll's husband to bear. Moll tried to persuade her husband that his credit was good and that the loss would not ruin him, but to no avail. He was so overcome by the event that he fell ill and died.

Again Moll had to face life alone with two children—only now she was forty-eight. She could no longer look forward to being a mistress; she had no friends, and little money. She lived two years in this condition, growing poorer each day. To reduce her expenses Moll sold the house and lived in rooms, and sold most of her furniture and linens. She lived for another year on that money, spending sparingly and eking out an existence.

In reflecting on this period of her life, Moll urges her readers to remember the prayer, "Give me not poverty, lest I steal." One day in her rather aimless wanderings, Moll passed an apothecary's shop where she saw a bundle on a stool and a servant with her back to it. After checking to see that no one was looking, Moll took the bundle and left. She was in a trance, and wandered around until nine o'clock that night. When she arrived home she opened the bundle and found some linen, silverware, silk handkerchiefs, and a little money. Suddenly struck by what she had done, she began to cry; she realized that she could be taken to Newgate Prison for her crime. After sleeping fitfully, she waited for news of the robbery but heard nothing of it. At first, Moll regretted her crime, for fear the person from whom she stole was as poor as she, but the longer she thought about her own condition, the harder her heart became. She reflected on her earlier repentance, her sober and retired life with the banker, and now—driven by necessity—the destruction of her soul. She fell on her knees praying, but soon realized that this repentance was not sincere.

After this, Moll had a great many thieving escapades. Once she even stole a necklace of gold beads from a child's neck after luring the little girl away. She prided herself on not doing bodily harm to the child and thought of her adventure as a lesson to the family for leaving the child unattended.

Another time, a man who was running with a bundle threw it near Moll and said, "God bless you, mistress, let it lie there a little." Soon two more men ran by, with several others in pursuit. Two escaped, but the other was caught. After the crowd had passed, Moll took the bundle and walked away. When she returned home, she found the bundle contained some silk and velvet. Because she "had only robbed the thief," Moll felt no remorse about this robbery.

Moll continued to steal, since so far she had had such good luck. Once, when she was walking around the town, she saw two rings lying on a window ledge inside a house. She thought to knock on the window; if anyone responded, she would warn the people to remove the rings since she "had seen two suspicious fellows take notice of them." But when no one answered her knocks, she broke the glass and took the rings.

Moll's problem now was that she did not know how to sell the things she stole. Therefore, she resolved to renew her friendship with an old acquaintance.

DISCUSSION

After Moll had been living a settled and contented life for five years, her means of support was suddenly snatched away in unusual circumstances. She again was alone with little means of support.

In Moll's account of her descent into crime, note her progression from a dream state, to horror, to rationalization, to fears, to attempts at reformation, repentance and prayers, to an eventual hardening of the heart.

QUESTION

In Chapter 14, Moll spoke of the way a person's good intentions can be turned, against his will, into evil actions. Explain why she feels this happened to her.

CHAPTER 16

SYNOPSIS: Adventures with the Midwife

The friendship Moll intended to renew was with the midwife, to whom she had sent £5 a year for the support of her child until, after the death of her banker husband, she became too poor to continue to do so. However, Moll had written a letter explaining that her husband had died and that she was unable to continue sending money for her child, and requested that the child not suffer because of her misfortunes.

Moll now paid a visit to her old "governess," as she called the midwife. While there, she learned that her governess still occasionally acted as a midwife, but that she had lost much of her trade and money because of a law suit brought against her by a man whose daughter the midwife had helped to run away from him. The incident had taken the midwife near the gallows, but she was still an enterprising woman and became a pawn-broker, living by this pretty well.

She received Moll kindly and told her that she could stop worrying about her son for he was well cared for. Moll showed the governess the silk, beads, and ring and asked for advice on how to get money for them. The governess said she could sell them because she had turned pawnbroker. This she did. Moll hoped that now her governess could help her make an honest living, but the governess knew of no way to do so. Moll was now past fifty and knew she needed a stable business.

The governess invited Moll to stay with her until she could find something to do. Further, Moll's governess made arrange-ments to have her son by the banker adopted at a cost of £5 a year. Moll was happy with her present circumstances and re-solved to make her living sewing, if she could get work. This was difficult, though, because Moll had few friends. Neverthe-less, she managed to get a little sewing and worked very hard. Soon, however, she felt the urge to steal again. Prompted by the urgings of "the diligent devil," she stole a silver tankard from a tavern and took it home. Wanting to test her governess, she pretended to her that, "without any design," she'd walked off with the tankard and now wondered what she should do about it. The governess convinced her not to return the tankard lest she be sent to Newgate Prison. The governess then told Moll it would be nice if she "could light of such a bargain once a week." Moll now learned that her governess quite frequently received stolen goods, and melted down plate in order to disguise it from its rightful owners. She did this with Moll's tankard and gave her its full value in money, though she never did this for the rest of her customers.

The governess soon talked Moll into becoming a full-time

thief and introduced her to a woman who taught her how to be much more skillful at shoplifting, stealing pocketbooks, and lifting watches from ladies' sides. Moll became this woman's apprentice, for some time practicing on the women herself. Soon Moll was sent out to steal a watch from a young lady. As the instructor bumped into the young lady, Moll lifted her watch and ran away; subsequently, the instructor told the young lady that the "rogues who thrust [her] down" must have stolen the watch.

This was the first time Moll had worked with an accomplice; together they did very well. Moll was now "a complete thief, hardened to a pitch above all the reflections of conscience or modesty," even though she no longer had need to fear being poor, since she was doing well with her needlework. Moll maintains, though, that if she had been able to get honest work when she had desperately needed it, she would not have returned to a life of crime. Success had now hardened her. She had shifted from need to greed.

The capture and execution of her accomplice made Moll more cautious, but did not make her stop stealing. Her governess, ever alert for opportunities, sent Moll to a burning house under the pretext of helping the occupants but with the actual intention of stealing what she could during the excitement. This Moll performed well and brought home rings, lockets, a watch, and money. For a brief time, Moll was remorseful about this particular thievery, but this feeling soon wore off; her greed had become too strong. She soon met other partners and continued her criminal activities.

The other accomplices were caught and hanged. Though Moll was inclined to be very cautious about stealing so often, she now had two prompters: the devil and her governess. Moll would make deals with custom-house officers to share in the value of goods that had been smuggled in and that Moll had learned about from her governess. At other times she would buy prohibited goods, and then betray the owners. Moll was now not only a thief but also a betrayer of thieves.

DISCUSSION

Notice how Moll focused on the circumstances which caused the midwife to become a pawnbroker and then a receiver of stolen goods. Note, too, that the bond between Moll and the midwife was becoming stronger. Moll occasionally called her "mother" and referred to her as "my governess."

As she has done before, Moll in this chapter shows the odd combination of calculated and deliberate criminality and an almost puritanical moralism.

QUESTIONS

Thinking carefully about the events in this chapter, who would you say takes the initiative in crime, Moll or her governess? Do you feel that Moll is being led into crime or are both women equally involved?

CHAPTER 17

SYNOPSIS: A Clever Escape and a Disguise

Once, Moll was almost caught as she tried to steal a gold watch from a lady. Using the techniques she had learned from her first accomplice, Moll discovered that the watch was too securely fastened to the lady's side. Realizing that she was in danger of being discovered, Moll herself called out, as though *she* had been "attempted" by pickpockets. Since Moll was very well-dressed, as was her custom when she was on these adventures, she was not suspected as the would-be thief. In fact, a young fellow a little farther in the crowd was caught in the act of pickpocketing and was seized by the crowd. This was a narrow escape for Moll, so she did not try stealing gold watches for a while.

Also, Moll discovered that her old governess had once been a pickpocket, had been caught, convicted, and ordered to transportation. She had managed to talk and buy her way into being put ashore in Ireland, where she had practiced her trade for a number of years. Then she had turned midwife and procuress, and had become "pretty well known." She had returned to England, and continued to prosper as a midwife until the lawsuit had stripped her of her wealth. It was through this woman's advice and help that Moll had been able, through her five years of stealing, to avoid the authorities at Newgate, although they had heard a lot about her.

One of Moll's greatest dangers was that she was too well-known by other thieves. She feared that, because of their envy of her never having been caught, they might betray her. Moll never knew why these thieves gave her the name of Moll Flanders. Although she had once gone by the name of Mrs. Flanders when she had hidden in the Mint, she felt that they did not know about this.

When she learned that some of those in Newgate were going to betray her, she remained indoors for a long while. Soon, however, due to her governess's impatience, Moll disguised herself as a man and continued stealing, with a young man as her new accomplice.

Because of the foolish daring of this accomplice, they were once nearly caught. He was pursued more intently than she, because he had the stolen goods. Moll ran into her governess's house, with a crowd in hot pursuit. While she discarded her disguise, her governess insisted to the crowd that no man had run into the house. When Moll was prepared, the governess opened the door and followed the men, who searched the house from top to bottom but found nothing out of order.

The young man who had been with Moll had his indictment deferred when he promised to give the name of his accomplice. He did so, but the name he gave was Gabriel Spencer; he knew nothing, in fact, about Moll, not even that she was a woman.

This whole incident frightened Moll so much that she left her governess for a while and went to Dunstable. There she spent five weeks with the couple who had been her landlady and landlord when she had lived there with her Lancashire husband. She made them believe she was to meet her husband at their house. While there, Moll received several letters from her governess, including one which said that Moll's young accomplice had been hanged. Moll told her landlady that she had received word from her husband to the effect that his business would not permit him to leave Ireland and that she had to return without him. With this she left.

DISCUSSION

Notice how Moll became slightly annoyed with her governess when the woman expressed dissatisfaction with Moll's suspension of criminal activities because she feared arrest. Moll made a point of saying that she took all the risks while her governess shared the profits. Here, too, Moll focused on the foolish risk her male partner had taken. This has implications for Moll's future criminal activities.

QUESTION

Why do you think Moll continued to steal, even though she feared arrest and prison?

CHAPTER 18

SYNOPSIS: Moll Finds a Suitor

After Moll's return to London, her governess said that she would never again recommend a partner to Moll, for she found Moll had better luck when she worked alone. Moll also felt she was safer relying on her own good sense rather than on others, who were often dull, rash, and impatient.

Moll thought about why she continued her crimes; the ''temptation of necessity'' was gone, since she now had almost £500. She realized that she was so hardened in crime that no fear affected her nor did the examples of the arrest, conviction, and hanging of her accomplices.

Moll recalled an earlier occasion when she had seen another accomplice arrested with the stolen goods on her: Moll had handed them to her as they left the shop and went their separate ways. Her cautious use of the pseudonym Moll Flanders and the concealment of her residence succeeded in obscuring her real identity, while her accomplice was caught and transported.

This event was what had led Moll to the use of men's clothes as a disguise. The disguise was soon discarded, though, because Moll found the clothes difficult to get about in and had been nearly caught in the disguise.

All of the witnesses against Moll were either hanged or transported; therefore, if Moll were arrested, she surmised she could assume a different name and thus reduce her sentence to that of a first offender. In view of this, she again became involved in crime.

During another fire near the governess's home, Moll became injured when a featherbed thrown from the burning house fell on her. Her injury and fear kept her home for a while.

When she recovered, Moll went to the Bartholomew Fair; there she met a gentleman in a raffle shop who liked her company.

Being somewhat drunk, he took Moll for a ride in a coach to the Spring Garden, where they walked in the gardens and he continued to drink. After their return to town, this gentleman took Moll to a house and made love to her. While they were returning in the coach, the gentleman fell asleep. Moll stole his gold watch, a silk purse of gold, his periwig and silver-fringed gloves, his sword, and his snuffbox; then she left the coach when it stopped to let another coach pass.

Moll, as usual, excused her deeds, putting the blame on the gentleman and saying that he probably had a virtuous wife and innocent children at home and would feel ashamed of his conduct when he became sober. She goes on at length to mock and abuse such gentlemen as the one she had just robbed.

Moll's governess was very much pleased with Moll's account of her adventures and schemed how to make the gentleman pay for the return of his stolen goods. After hearing Moll's very complete description of the man, the governess said she thought she knew who he was. She snooped around and discovered that the man she suspected, a baronet of a very good family, had indeed been robbed and then beaten, presumably by his coachman. The governess arranged a meeting with the gentleman and assured him that the lady he had been with knew nothing of his identity and that she was "a gentlewoman, and no woman of the town." At first reluctant to admit that he had been with Moll, the gentleman finally asked to see her again, but the governess refused. She offered instead to return any of his possessions that he wanted. In time, she returned them to him and received much more than she would have been able to get by pawning them. Because the gentleman persisted in his inquiry after Moll, the governess finally persuaded Moll to see him. The affair continued for about a year, during which Moll refrained from stealing since she was being somewhat supported by the gentleman.

DISCUSSION

Here again Moll explains why she preferred to work alone. Nevertheless, she often worked with accomplices. Recall that all of the witnesses against Moll were either hanged or transported. In England the crime of stealing was punishable by death or indentured servitude. An indentured servant is a person bound by a written contract or agreement to service in a colony.

Poverty and greed were factors which Moll said made her continue stealing. Nevertheless, she curtailed her criminal activities when she formed an attachment with a gentleman.

QUESTION

Do you see any relationship between Moll's stealing and her ceasing to steal when she attaches herself to a man?

CHAPTER 19

SYNOPSIS: A Return to Crime

A few months after the relationship terminated, Moll returned to her old trade. Disguised as an ordinary working woman, she waited outside an inn which was used as a stopping place for several stage-coaches. Servants would come to the inn and give various parcels and bundles to the coachmen to take to their employers in the country. Moll had the opportunity to be entrusted with a bundle of goods by a servant, who then went off in search of her mistress. As soon as the servant had gone, Moll removed her apron, wrapped the bundle and her straw hat in the apron, and then put the bundle on her head. Thus she escaped detection when the woman who had given her the bundle passed by. Moll took the bundle, which contained some good cloth and lace, home to her governess. Since Moll had had such a successful adventure, she was given encouragement by her governess to try this criminal technique on several other occasions in different places.

It was not long after these various adventures that Moll finally became known to the authorities. While disguised as a widow, Moll heard the cry of "Stop thief!" Though for once Moll was not involved in any crime, the mob mistook her for the real thief, another woman dressed as a widow, and gathered around her. Although the shopkeeper said she was not the thief, Moll was kept for almost an hour waiting for the journeyman to return to identify her.

Meanwhile, the servants were very rude to Moll. The shopowner refused to say Moll had stolen from him, but he would not let her go or send for friends. She, therefore, became very annoyed and said she would enter a counter charge. Moll asked the constable to call for a porter to bring her a pen, ink, and paper. She was refused this request. Then Moll asked the porter his name and address and told him to be a witness to how she was being treated. The porter asked for proof that the shopowner would not release Moll. Moll inquired in a loud voice for him to do so; he refused. The porter agreed to bear witness to this interchange. After watching this scene, the constable wanted to release Moll, but the shopowner taunted him, "Are you a justice of peace or a constable? I charged you with her; pray do your duty." Finally, the journeyman returned with the real thief and the shopowner apologized to Moll. She, however, insisted on some sort of "reparation" for her humiliation and harsh treatment, and wanted to be taken to a magistrate. At this the journeyman and the constable fell to quarreling and fighting; during the confusion, the real thief escaped—as Moll herself had so often done in the past.

When the group finally appeared before the judge, and the constable had given a summary of the scene, Moll was asked her name; reluctantly, she said that she was Mary Flanders and that she lived with her governess, whose name she also gave. Then she proceeded to tell how she had been abused and mistreated and how the real thief had been caught and then lost. The constable, the shopowner, and the journeyman told their accounts of what had happened. The consequence of all this was that Moll was released and the journeyman was sent to Newgate for striking the constable.

After this Moll went home to her governess. The governess saw much humor in the story, informed Moll that she was a lucky woman, and encouraged her to sue the shopowner for £500 in damages and to sue the journeyman as well.

Because she had given her name to the justice of peace and

because that name was so well-known to authorities and criminals alike, Moll feared an open trial for damages. The governess, though, found an attorney with a good reputation to take the case. The shopowner wanted to settle the case out of court and asked Moll's attorney to persuade her to do likewise. After haggling over the amount, Moll finally accepted £150, a suit of black silk clothes, and payment of the attorney's fees. The shopowner begged Moll to drop her charges against the journeyman, saying that the man would be ruined by the suit. Moll "generously" agreed to forget the matter.

DISCUSSION

In Chapter 17, we learned that Moll was known to the authorities only by the name, Moll Flanders, that had been given her by other criminals. By using disguises and fictitious names she had been able to avoid detection. Here we see that Moll had to appear before a judge and give her name. She gave the name of Mary Flanders, Moll being a diminutive of Mary.

QUESTION

What do you think will be the consequences of Moll's having given her name to the judge?

CHAPTER 20

SYNOPSIS: A New Disguise

Because of her most recent activities, Moll now had £700 in money besides clothes, rings, some plate, and two gold watches. There was no need for her to continue her evil ways, but greed forced her on. Since her near-capture in widow's clothes, Moll decided to change her disguise to that of a beggar woman.

One time when she was standing near a tavern door, a gentleman got off his horse, asked a servant to hold it, and went into the tavern. Shortly thereafter, the servant's master called him and seeing no one but Moll, he asked her to hold the horse. She agreed, and took it to her governess. Neither woman knew what to do with the horse; "never was poor thief more at a loss to know what to do with anything that was stolen." Finally, they had the horse taken to another tavern and sent a note to the owner telling him that the poor lady who had held the horse had not been able to lead him back to the right tavern. This then was a theft and no theft.

While Moll was still disguised as a beggar she met some counterfeiters who frightened her so much she decided to discard her beggar's disguise so that they could not find her again and perhaps murder her to assure them their secret.

As Moll stated, counterfeiting, horse-stealing, and house-breaking were not in her line; her trade was in another direction. Though risky, it was more suitable to her and allowed more chances for escape.

Soon Moll met a woman who had success on the dock by stealing smuggled goods. She joined the woman in several adventures. Later, when Moll tried it alone, she had no success and so gave it up.

Moll's next adventure involved a different disguise. She dressed in fine clothes and walked to the other end of town where she had an opportunity to steal some lace while a crowd of people were distracted by news that the Queen was approaching. Moll escaped by shutting herself up in a coach minutes before she heard cries of "robbed" and "lace."

The next day she wore a different outfit of fine clothes and walked in the Mall in St. James Park, where she saw many elegant ladies. She also saw two little girls, aged about twelve and nine. The older girl wore a fine gold watch and a good pearl necklace. As soon as the young ladies had walked on a bit, Moll asked their footman many questions about the girls; then she went up to the children and spoke to them so familiarly that they assumed Moll was a friend of the family. While Moll and the girls were walking and talking, a crowd gathered to see the King go by on his way to the Parliament Houses. As Moll lifted both girls up so they could see, she was carefully removing the gold watch. She then hastened away, after telling the older girl to take care of her little sister.

Moll next had an adventure quite different from all the rest. This one was at a gaming-house near Covent Garden. She gambled with money given her by a gentleman there, and repeatedly won for him. Soon Moll began easing some of the money into her own pocket. At the end, Moll gave him all of the money in sight, half of which he returned to her. From this adventure, Moll returned home with seventy-three guineas. When she told her governess about this adventure, Moll was cautioned against doing it again for fear she might get the itch to gamble.

Since Moll and her governess had done so well financially, the governess felt they should stop and be satisfied with what they had. Moll resisted this suggestion: since she had escaped capture, she "grew more hardened and audacious than ever." She felt pride that her name was as famous as that of any thief of her type who had ever been at Newgate or Old Bailey.

DISCUSSION

Moll acknowledges that she had no need to continue stealing because she was the richest thief in England. She was not yet ready to repent, but instead adopted new disguises. In her pride, she was becoming increasingly daring and reckless.

In this chapter, Moll stole a horse for which she had no use. Stealing the horse became a symbol of her degradation.

QUESTION

Moll seems unable to give up her life of thieving, which is a kind of gambling. Why do you think she was able to stop "real" gambling after just one time?

CHAPTER 21

SYNOPSIS: Capture

It was now a time of year when the gentlemen usually left town, leaving few occasions for Moll's type of adventures. She joined a gang and went to Stourbridge Fair and Bury Fair in Suffolk. Since there were slim pickings there, she soon tired of the whole business and went off alone.

During the course of Moll's subsequent crimes, she stole a heavy trunk from a drunken Dutch footman. She contrived to have the trunk taken on board a boat that was sailing to Ipswich, and she told her landlady she was going to London. She even managed to fool the custom-house officers in Ipswich by telling them—since she suspected that the trunk contained a man's clothes only—that her husband had the key. When they broke open the lock, they were therefore not surprised to find that it did indeed contain a man's clothes. Moll subsequently removed what she wanted from the trunk, left it with the landlady at an inn, and found a ride to Colchester. There she inquired after her old friends and discovered that her first "parents" and brother-in law were dead. From Colchester, Moll returned to London,where she recounted her adventures to her governess. Here Moll pauses in her story to warn honest people among her readers to keep their wits about them: otherwise, persons such as herself will take advantage of them.

On the evening of Christmas Day, Moll passed an open but empty silversmith's shop, with a good deal of plate in the window. Just as she was about to take it, a fellow who lived across the street and who had seen her enter the empty shop came running in. Just as he was about to seize her, Moll had the presence of mind to stamp on the floor and call out for the owner. Her story about trying to match a spoon (which, "by great luck," she had in her pocket) was convincing enough for her to be deemed innocent by an alderman who was among the crowd that had been attracted by the noise. However, Moll then had to buy the spoons she had said she was looking for. The narrow escape did not slow Moll down, however, and three days later she was caught by two women in a linen shop as she tried to leave with some stolen cloth. This time the constable refused to accept her story and took her straight to Newgate.

DISCUSSION

In this chapter Moll makes a point of saying that her story may be useful to honest people. She warns them to keep their wits about them in order to guard against strangers like herself. She says her history has a moral and she leaves it to the reader to "let the experience of one creature completely wicked, and completely miserable, be a storehouse of useful warning to those that read."

It is evident that the several times that Moll almost got captured did not make her more cautious. She was past caution now. Her degradation was complete, so her capture was imminent and inevitable.

QUESTION

Moll has managed to survive all sorts of misfortunes; how do you think she'll manage in Newgate, a place she has dreaded all her life?

CHAPTER 22

SYNOPSIS: Newgate Prison

The very name of Newgate sent chills through Moll's body. This was the place where so many of her accomplices and comrades had been sent, from where many were hanged; this was the place where her mother had been housed, and where she herself had been born and where she feared she would die.

The noise, the odors, and the crowd terribly distressed Moll. She now reproached herself repeatedly for having continued her criminal activities in spite of her many narrow escapes and her more-than-sufficient money. She did not reproach herself because she had sinned against God and man, but because she had been caught.

Her arrival at Newgate was greeted by a great uproar from the inmates, for she was the most notorious among them. They scorned her for having been captured: "What! Mrs. Flanders come to Newgate at last? What! Mrs. Mary, Mrs. Molly, and after that plain Moll Flanders?"

That night Moll sent news of her capture to her old governess, who was quite upset by it. The next morning she came to see Moll and comforted her as best she could. After this the governess found the women who had caught Moll, and tried to bribe them not to appear against her. Neither would take her bribes. She then appealed to the man whose goods had been stolen and to his wife. They were too much afraid to withdraw the charges against Moll. Thus, Moll lived many days at Newgate with constant fears of death. The longer she stayed, the harder she became. "I degenerated into stone." She felt neither remorse nor repentance despite the fact that she was sure her sentence would be death since she was an old offender. She lost heart and had no thought for escape.

While Moll was in this apathetic state, she heard that three highwaymen had been brought into the prison. When Moll got a chance to see the men, she discovered that one was her Lancashire husband, Jemmy. She became speechless at the sight of him and was relieved that he did not know her. She retired to meditate upon this turn of events and blamed his misfortunes on her having married him under false pretenses. She grieved day and night for him.

Moll learned that she would soon be sentenced. Her hard shell fell off and she began to meditate again. This made her even more distressed and dejected than when she had arrived. In this state Moll sent for her old governess, who tried, unsuccessfully, to bribe the jurymen. For the first time in a long while, Moll prayed—but she still expressed no real sorrow or repentance for her crimes.

At her arraignment, Moll pleaded not guilty; the following day she was brought to trial and was found guilty of felony, but acquitted of burglary. However, the felony alone carried the death sentence. Despite Moll's plea for mercy, the sentence of death was pronounced upon her.

The governess was terribly upset: disconsolate about Moll's sentence and penitent about her own sins. She arranged for a minister to visit Moll, and Moll spent two days telling him about her wicked life. Moll said, "It was now that for the first time, I felt any real signs of repentance. . . . The word eternity represented itself with all its incomprehensible additions." Because the minister believed Moll, he worked to get her a reprieve. Later he managed to have her sentence changed to transportation, "which indeed was a hard condition in itself, but not when comparatively considered."

Moll's governess had been made very ill by the news of Moll's sentence of death. When she recovered she came to the prison and, learning of the new sentence, hinted that there might be a way around it: Moll might be able to buy her way out of transportation.

DISCUSSION

When Moll was taken to prison she at first seemed to repent, but she merely regretted her imprisonment. She seemed more sincere in her sorrow about Jemmy's imprisonment. Notice that throughout this personal history, Moll takes no responsibility for her acts. She blames her evil ways on her innocence, her poverty, her greed, her governess, the devil, or fate.

Defoe's vivid account of Newgate Prison indicates his familiarity with the place. His descriptions of the people there are probably based on the prisoners he met when he spent several months there in 1703.

Note Moll's explanation of how her constant contact with the other prisoners made her "first stupid and senseless, then brutish and thoughtless, and at last raving mad as any of them were."

QUESTION
Why do you think Moll's governess remains so loyal to her?

CHAPTER 23

SYNOPSIS: Reunion

Fifteen weeks later Moll was put on board a ship in the Thames with a group of thirteen hardened criminals. Between the time that the order for transportation was given and the time that Moll was put on board the ship, she learned that Jemmy, her Lancashire husband, and one of his companions had been able to buy off some of the witnesses against them, but that they were still being held to see if any other witnesses would appear against them. By pretending to be a witness against Jemmy, Moll contrived to see him alone. After the keeper left, they exchanged confidences about their years apart: Moll told him as much as "was convenient" about her arrest and imprisonment; Jemmy explained that in all his twenty-five years of highway robbery he'd never before been caught, although he'd often been wounded. Moll began trying to persuade Jemmy to attempt to get transportation to the colonies, but he had given up all hope and wished to die. He continued for some time to resist Moll's arguments, but she finally "answered all his own passionate objections so effectually" that he agreed to try to arrange for transportation. A "great friend" interceded on Jemmy's behalf and he was granted permission to "transport himself." Moll was upset by this piece of news, for she feared that she and Jemmy would not be transported on the same ship.

As the date for Moll's transportation drew near, her governess tried to obtain a pardon for her, but did not have enough money to bring this off. The minister also tried but was told that Moll's life had been saved because of his entreaties and he should not ask for more.

When Moll was "delivered" to the ship of "a merchant that traded to Virginia," she was terrified that the boat was going to leave immediately. Soon reassured on this matter, she wrote a letter to her governess and enclosed one for a "fellow-prisoner," whom she did not let her governess know was her husband. Moll told the governess where the ship was and urged the woman to send along any of Moll's things she could get together.

The governess gave the letter to Jemmy and got an answer to it. The next day she came down to the ship and brought Moll the letter along with a chest containing some money and many other goods.

Jemmy's letter said he did not see how he could be discharged in time to go to Virginia in the same ship with Moll. This news distressed Moll so much that she told her governess some details of the problem. She also said Jemmy had some money and that they planned to be married on board ship.

This news pleased the governess to the extent that she finally managed to have Jemmy brought on board the ship. Now both Jemmy and Moll were on their way to Virginia, "destined to be sold for slaves, [Moll] for five years, and he under bonds and security not to return to England any more, as long as he lived."

DISCUSSION

Although Moll was already on the ship at the beginning of this chapter, the scene flashes back to the time of the renewal of the friendship between Moll and Jemmy in prison. When they met, Jemmy gave Moll a full account of the circumstances of their first meeting, his resolve to stop stealing, his disappointment with her meager fortune (but not with her), and his criminal activities up to the time of his arrest.

QUESTION
Why do you think Moll lies to Jemmy about her career as a thief and about her arrest?

CHAPTER 24

SYNOPSIS: The Trip to Virginia

The first thing Moll and Jemmy did was to take account of their belongings. Jemmy said that he had only £108 left. The rest of his stock had been used so he could live like a gentleman while in prison, solicit his case, and make friends. Moll's stock came to about £246, thus giving them a total of £354 between them. Unfortunately, their stock was all in money, "which every one knows is an unprofitable cargo to be carried to the plantations." Moll had left between £700 and £800 in the bank and £300 with her governess. Many of her clothes, jewels, and linens she had shipped to Virginia, to be delivered to her there under her real name.

By giving money to the boatswain and the captain, Moll saw to it that she and Jemmy were treated better than most of the other prisoners; indeed, the captain arranged for them to have a cabin and to eat at his table.

Moll's governess arranged for the captain to help her "two cousins," as she called Moll and Jemmy, obtain their freedom when they got to Virginia. She also asked what planter's tools and materials were needed; these she bought and had put on board in her own name, endorsing them over to Jemmy, who gave her his £108, in addition to "a good sum" that Moll paid.

During the time the ship was still in port, the captain took Moll and Jemmy on shore with him for dinner with his wife and Moll's old governess.

Finally the ship set sail and after forty-two days arrived at the coast of Virginia. The captain told Moll she must get somebody there to buy them as servants and to answer for them to the governor of the country. Moll agreed to this arrangement and the captain brought a planter to purchase them as servants. They went to shore with him and soon afterward the planter gave them "a certificate of discharge, and an acknowledgement of having served him faithfully"; they were free the next morning to go wherever they wished. Moll and Jemmy bought "six thousand weight of tobacco" for the captain and gave him twenty guineas besides for his services to them.

DISCUSSION

Notice that Moll was as resourceful as ever. In spite of her predicament, she managed to have her goods and husband with her, enjoy the conveniences of the ship, and obtain tools for their plantation in America.

QUESTION

What type of welcome do you think Moll will have from her family in America?

CHAPTER 25

SYNOPSIS: A New Life

Moll and Jemmy had their goods placed in a warehouse. Then Moll inquired after her mother and her brother, who was once her husband. She discovered that her mother had died, but that her brother was still alive, information which brought her no pleasure. Worse still, Moll learned that he no longer lived on the plantation where the three of them had once lived, but now lived with one of his sons near the very warehouse where Moll and Jemmy had stored their belongings.

Moll decided to cautiously take a look at the plantation and see her brother, since she felt sure he would not now recognize her. She met a woman who pointed out the plantation, and Moll proceeded toward the place. The woman also pointed out the owner, whom Moll knew to be her son, and the old gentleman, who was once her husband. She felt a mixture of joy and fright upon seeing them, but then realized she did not need to be so cautious since the old gentleman was nearly blind. Moll suddenly understood how terrible it was for a mother to see her son pass by and not be able to speak to him. Moll threw herself on the ground weeping and kissed the spot where her son had walked.

The woman, perceiving Moll's troubled condition and acting to divert her, told her the story about the two gentlemen. It was, of course, a story quite familiar to Moll, for it was about her own life with her mother and brother. Moll was quite moved by the account, but acted astonished so that she could question the woman for further details. Moll learned that her mother had left her some money and her plantation, in trust with her grandson. Now Moll wondered how and when, or even whether, she should make herself known so as to collect her inheritance.

Jemmy perceived that Moll was very worried about something and insisted that she tell him about it. Therefore, Moll was forced to tell him some part of the story.

DISCUSSION

Events seem to be moving in Moll's favor, if she could only clear up the problem of her brother.

QUESTION

Does Moll's rush of maternal feeling seem believable and in character?

CHAPTER 26

SYNOPSIS: A New Lie

The story Moll told Jemmy varied somewhat from the truth. She told him they would have to move since she had discovered that, although her mother was dead, some of her relatives lived quite close to them and Moll did not feel it would be proper for these relatives to know the circumstances of her coming to America. Jemmy agreed with Moll.

How to collect her inheritance was still a problem which caused Moll many worried moments. Her worries in turn distressed and annoyed Jemmy, for he felt Moll was not being completely truthful.

Moll expresses her realization of how heavy the weight of keeping a secret can be on anyone. She digresses in her story to tell the reader that neither man nor woman of high or low character or circumstance can bear alone the heavy weight of a secret.

She gives several examples to prove her point. For instance, while she was in Newgate Prison, Moll had met a man known as a night-flyer. This criminal would talk in his sleep and reveal his crimes to such an extent that he had to lock himself in at night or pay someone to lock him in. Moll felt that if he had been able to tell his secrets to anyone, he would have been able to sleep.

Moll returns to her own account by saying to the reader that the only relief she found was in telling her husband enough of her story to convince him of the necessity for leaving that part of the country.

The next problem was to decide on what part of the country to move to. Maryland, Pennsylvania, East and West Jersey, New York, and New England, which all lay north of Virginia, were out because Moll had an aversion to cold climates, particularly now that she was old. She decided to go to Carolina because it was the only southern colony which belonged to England. She realized also how easy it would be to return to Virginia as soon as she felt it was safe to collect her inheritance.

DISCUSSION

Moll's problems seem to be getting more complicated. If she stayed in Virginia, there was a danger of meeting her brother. If she left, she might not be able to claim her inheritance.

Notice that Moll missed having a confidant to tell her thoughts to. Her governess had filled this function for many years.

QUESTION
Why can't Moll tell Jemmy her secrets?

CHAPTER 27

SYNOPSIS: Another Problem

The new problem had to do with the fact that Moll was reluctant to leave Virginia without making some claim to her inheritance. Nor could she bear the thought of leaving without making herself known to her brother or to her son. However, she didn't want Jemmy to know anything of them, and *vice versa*.

Moll considered sending Jemmy to Carolina with all their goods and following him later, but discarded this idea because she knew he would not go without her. Then she considered leaving with him for Carolina and taking part of their goods, only to return to Virginia alone for the rest; but she knew he would never let her return without him.

The problems seemed insurmountable because in addition to the above, Moll was afraid if she did not hurry and identify herself to her brother, he might die and it might be impossible for her to convince her son of her true identity and her right to her inheritance. Yet, Moll did not see fit to reveal to them that she had been brought over from England as a criminal or that she had another husband with her.

Moll continued telling Jemmy of the absolute necessity for not settling where they then were, for fear their criminal pasts might be revealed. She also explained that she had reason to believe that her mother had left her something but that it was dangerous to inquire about it at that time. Moll suggested that after they were settled in Carolina, she would visit her relations and inquire about her inheritance; she felt sure that by then she would be received with respect since she and Jemmy would have some money. Otherwise, she might be subjected to all kinds of affronts and legal suits which she knew would be painful to him. With these arguments, Moll convinced Jemmy that they should go to Carolina.

DISCUSSION

Remember that Moll was supposed to serve time as an indentured servant. She had had her goods shipped to her in Virginia under her real name. Moll was truly afraid of any great notice being taken of her and Jemmy. If this were not the case, we can assume that Moll would not have hesitated to try immediately to collect her inheritance.

QUESTION

How do you think Moll will arrange to collect her inheritance without revealing her criminal past or her relationship to Jemmy?

CHAPTER 28

SYNOPSIS: A Home at Last

After a number of inquiries, Moll and Jemmy learned that a ship had arrived in Maryland from Carolina and would be returning soon. Therefore, they hired a sloop to take their possessions to Maryland.

The voyage was a long and unpleasant one, and much worse than the trip from England because the weather was unpleasant and the ship small. In addition, the river was so broad that they could not see the shore on either side. Moll worried that they might lose their lives—or keep their lives while losing their goods—leaving them destitute in a wild, strange place without friends.

Five days later, however, they arrived in Maryland, only to discover that the ship bound for Carolina had left three days earlier. Nevertheless, since the land in Maryland was fertile and good, they decided to settle there.

When they landed they met an honest Quaker who directed them to a place near the mouth of the Chesapeake Bay. Here, they bought two servants, one an English woman-servant and the other a Negro man-servant, absolute necessities for people who intended to settle there. The Quaker helped in the purchase and also led Moll and Jemmy to convenient lodgings.

In two months' time they bought a large piece of land from the governor of Maryland.

A year later they had almost "fifty acres of land cleared, part of it enclosed, and some of it planted with tobacco." They also had a garden and sufficient corn "to help supply [their] servants with roots and herbs and bread."

Moll was now able to convince her husband to let her return to Virginia. He was willing to do so since he had work enough to do, as well as hunting to occupy his leisure time.

DISCUSSION

In a year's time Moll and Jemmy had a profitable plantation. The fact that Moll had remained out of prison so long attests to her management skills. It seems quite possible that if she had put as much effort into making an honest living before this, she could have done so.

QUESTION

Does it seem likely that Moll and Jemmy would be so successful so quickly? Be specific in supporting your answer.

CHAPTER 29

SYNOPSIS: A Reunion

Moll "resolved to go up point-blank" to her brother and tell him who she was; then she decided to write him a letter first to identify herself and to assure him that she meant to give him no trouble about the old relationship, but wanted merely to ask his help in securing what their mother had left her. In her letter, Moll spoke well of his son and said that she would appreciate being allowed to see him.

Moll felt that her brother would probably ask their son to read the letter, since he himself was nearly blind. The son did receive the letter and did read it. Then he asked the messenger to show him the lady who had sent the letter. The messenger pointed to Moll. With this, Moll's son came up to kiss and embrace her. Then he began to sob. Moll felt great joy at this and they both cried for a long time. At last the son said that he had never expected to see her alive.

After both had recovered, the son told Moll that he had not shown her letter to his father, who was old, ill, and almost blind. The son felt that it would not be wise to put this business in his father's hands. Moll was pleased to find her son such a sensible young man. She explained that she could understand his father's condition, since her decision to leave him had left him somewhat infirm in body and mind. Moll recounted so many facts about her life in Virginia with his father and grandmother that she left her son no doubt that she was truly his mother.

Moll also told her son that she was living in Maryland at the plantation of a friend who had come from England in the same ship with her. The son invited Moll to live with him, assuring her that his father would never guess who she was. Moll pretended to consider the arrangement and then told her son that, though she did not wish to live apart from him, she could not bring herself to live with his father and be forever reminded of the past, or be under restraint for fear of being discovered by his father. The son acknowledged the wisdom of this and took Moll on horseback to a plantation next to his own. Referring to Moll as his aunt, he left word with the tenants to take good care of her. Two hours later he sent servants and dinner. Moll had a momentary regret that she had brought her "Lancashire husband" from England; however, she soon disposed of this thought for she really loved Jemmy.

Early the next morning the son brought her some money and his grandmother's will and read it to her. Moll discovered that her mother had left her a small plantation complete with servants and cattle. The son had hired a steward to run the place in Moll's absence and went over it himself about four times a year to check on it. He did the same for his father's plantation.

Moll asked the plantation's value and was told £60 a year if she rented it out, but at least £150 if she lived on it. The son said he would continue to manage it if she decided to return to Maryland or to England, and he felt he could assure her of £100 a year.

Moll was suddenly struck by all the good luck which had come her way and reproached herself for having done evil while Providence was returning good. With this, Moll told her son to have a will drawn up giving himself the plantation after her death. Further, she asked why he had not married and he told her wives were scarce and asked her to send one from London if she returned there.

During Moll's five-week stay in Virginia, he visited her every day. When the will was drawn up and signed, she prepared to leave. Before she did so, however, her son gave her £100 from the current year's crop.

DISCUSSION

Note that in spite of Moll's great love for Jemmy, she momentarily wished that she had not brought him from England, after receiving such wonderful treatment from her son.

QUESTION

What would you say is the reason Moll is beginning to have such good fortune?

CHAPTER 30

SYNOPSIS: More Good Fortune

Two days later, Moll arrived at her Quaker friend's home. She brought with her, for use on her plantation, many gifts from her son including horses, hogs, and cows. When she reached home she told her husband everything except that her cousin, as she called him, was actually her son. She explained the arrangements about the management of the plantation, and Jemmy was so touched and thankful that Moll believed he was truly a penitent and reformed man. At this point in the story, Moll explains that she could write volumes about their reformed selves but she doubts that such books would be as interesting as the account of their wickedness.

After this she returns to her own story, telling the reader that they continued managing their plantation and adding to their stock of money.

During the second year in America, Moll wrote to her old governess, telling her about the joy of their success, and asking her to send Moll's money to her in goods. This the old governess did, sending Moll and Jemmy a good supply of clothes, wigs, swords, fowling-pieces, a saddle with holsters and pistols, a cloak—everything Moll thought would make Jemmy appear the fine gentleman she felt him to be. In addition, they received iron-work, harness for the horses, tools, and clothes for servants. The governess also sent them three servant-women.

Jemmy was amazed by all these goods, and Moll finally told him of the money she had left behind in the bank and with her governess. When Moll asked him what he made of it all, Jemmy declared, "Make of it? . . . Why, who says I was deceived when I married a wife in Lancashire? I think I have married a fortune, and a very good fortune too."

In eight years the plantation was worth £300 annually. One year after her first visit, Moll went again to see her son, in order to collect the yearly income from her Virginia plantation. She was surprised to learn that her brother was dead, but she admits that this was not unpleasant news. Before she left her son, she told him that she thought she might remarry. Again she left with many presents.

Shortly thereafter, Moll let her son know she was married. Then she told Jemmy the truth about her son, and explained the events surrounding their relationship. Jemmy was "perfectly easy" about the story, and joined Moll in inviting her son to visit them.

Moll and Jemmy lived a happy and comfortable life together. Moll concludes her story:

> We are now grown old; I am come back to England, being almost seventy years of age, my husband sixty-eight, having performed much more than the limited terms of my transportation; and now, notwithstanding all the fatigues and all the miseries we have both gone through, we are both of us in good heart and health. My husband remained there some time after me to settle our affairs, and at first I had intended to go back to him, but at his desire I altered that resolution, and he is come over to England also, where we resolve to spend the remainder of our years in sincere penitence for the wicked lives we have lived.

DISCUSSION

In this chapter we see how thoroughly Moll believed in Jemmy's penitence and reformation. She felt that she could fill a larger history than the story of her life with proof of this fact, but she realized that it would probably go unread. Here Moll presents an indictment of the public for their preference for books about wickedness over those about goodness.

QUESTION

What do you think of Moll's resolutions to live "in sincere penitence" for the rest of her life? Do they contain any depth or sincerity?

CRITICAL ANALYSIS

AUTHOR

Many of the descriptions given in *Moll Flanders* are tautly drawn because of Defoe's personal experience with poverty and imprisonment. They are vivid and accurate accounts seemingly based on total recall of incidents and people he met. Later his confinement in Newgate Prison provided him with detailed encounters with thieves and their various thieving techniques, which he probably took down in his own version of shorthand during his interviews with them.

STRUCTURE

Moll Flanders is characterized by its episodic quality. Events follow events spasmodically with little or no transition. Incidents are arbitrarily held together with such weak transitions as "I had now a new scene of life upon my hands. . . ." or "At length a new scene opened." The phrases "in short" and "in a word" are used repeatedly to loosely tie one episode to another. Note how this occurs in the following passages: "The Captain's lady, in short, put this project . . ."; "in short, we were married, . . ."; "To bring the story short, we agreed to go."; "To make this part of the story short, . . ."; ". . . in short, it put him in a fit something like an apoplex; . . ."; "In short, by an unwearied importunity . . ."; (and again three on one page) "In short, I carried on the argument against this so far, . . ."; "In short, I ventured to avoid signing a contract of marriage, . . ."; and "In a word, I avoided a contract; . . ." The story unravels as a series of loosely connected episodes. There is, however, underlying continuity in the gradual unfolding of Moll's character.

Coincidence plays a large part in the work. Moll just happens to see an unattended bundle in an apothecary's shop and steals it when she is in low financial circumstances. This begins her life in crime. The governess, once a midwife, has just turned pawnbroker and therefore knows how to turn Moll's thieving into profit for them both. Jemmy happens to get arrested when Moll is in Newgate where they meet again after being many years apart. He happens to be transported to America on the same boat even after their frantic arrangements to expedite this fail.

The autobiographical method allows us to see Moll through her own eyes as she unfolds her account of events in her life.

CHARACTERIZATION

Moll's vanity and greed are the main focus of the characterization in the novel. Quite early in her life she has an all-consuming desire to become a gentlewoman, a fact which was almost impossible for a lower-class woman because of the rigid class lines in England in that period. In a sense this desire throughout her life leads her into one misadventure after another.

Moll's genteel education is beyond her "station in life" with its concentration on music, French and writing rather than on a vocational skill that could help her earn a living. To compound Moll's problem, she is excessively vain. From the time she is ten she hears herself referred to as pretty. Moll's initial seduction is as much the result of her vanity as the fine words and devious ways of the elder brother. She indicates, "That gentleman had now fired *his* inclinations as much as he had *my* vanity."

Defoe reveals Moll as an avaricious woman who sees people, even her own children, in economic terms. Gold is the thing that motivates the bulk of her actions, and the only deficits she experiences are emotional ones.

Defoe clearly reveals the difference between Moll's recurrent but passing misgivings about her degeneration, and her real repentance. Her repeated "considerations" but continuing "adventures" show Moll as essentially untouched emotionally and morally.

None of the other characters are vividly portrayed in this book. They simply serve to reflect Moll. They are a backdrop to her actions. In fact, these other characters seem rather unreal, shallow representations often remaining nameless, such as the elder brother, the "nurse," the governess, the Captain's widow, the ship's captain. Moll's mother is another nameless character. Most of her husbands and lovers are known by their trades or station in life such as the draper, the gentleman at Bath, the Lancashire husband.

THEMES
Greed

The major recurrent theme in the novel is that of greed— a greed which leads Moll to prostitution, thievery, and moral disintegration. Moll sees people as commodities—her relationships with them as business transactions. Although she is in love with the eldest brother, she has few qualms about taking money from him. She then accepts a bribe from him to marry his brother Robin. She easily consigns her children to the care of their grandparents and considers herself lucky. "My two children were, indeed, taken happily off of my hands by my husband's father and mother, . . ."She chooses husbands on the basis of their affluence or social class. When the first one dies she muses, "I had preserved the elder brother's bonds to me to pay me £500, which he offered me for my consent to marry his brother; and this, with what I saved of the money he formerly gave me and about as much more by my husband, left me a widow with about £1200 in my pocket." She takes money for prostitution. She steals from children and from people in distress. And only when she is too old to do otherwise does she repent.

It appears that Defoe consciously manipulates the reader to view Moll as a covetous individual. The terms he uses in the novel are very often economic, with direct recordings of Moll's business and criminal transactions. In journalistic fashion, Defoe itemizes the booty of Moll's first criminal venture:". . . I found there was a suit of childbed-linen in it, very good and almost new, the lace very fine; there was a silvery porringer of a pint, a small silver mug and six spoons, with some other linen, a good smock, and three silk handkerchiefs, and in the mug, in a paper, 18s.6d, in money."

In fact, at nearly any point in the book, the reader is able to approximate what is Moll's economic standing. Unfortunately, our knowledge of her inner life suffers. Kenneth Rexroth notes, "Moll Flanders has no interior life at all, and the material facts with which her character is constructed do not increase her individuality. They are chosen as facets of her typicality."

Defoe, in the Preface, insists that he is writing the book as a moral lesson to "give the history of a moral life repented. . . ." But Moll seems to flourish in her life of crime and actually the lesson we learn is that to survive one must fight with the weapons one has. Defoe was writing in a new, capitalistically oriented England. To have played the genteel lady would have meant a life of poverty for Moll. This was a decision which the social environment of the day forced on many people; Moll Flanders can be considered a good example of the criminal of that time who is forced into a life of crime by social conditions which leave few other alternatives. We cannot, thus, consider them too harshly for they are protagonists in the constant battle for survival which society imposes on the poor.

Vanity

An important theme of *Moll Flanders* is that vanity is the force that prevails over virtue. It is vanity that determines Moll's behavior in the first part of the book. Moll's vanity facilitates her seduction by the elder brother. It is also a strong motif which runs through Moll's five marriages and numerous lovers. It is a factor which precipitates her decision to steal rather than remain poor and exist only by the honest labor of her needle. In fact all her actions are in some way linked to her vanity.

Repentance

The theme of repentance is a recurring one in *Moll Flanders*. She constantly entertains the desire to repent. Lacking true moral persuasion these repentances are, until the end, half-hearted and insincere. She lacks moral strength; her moral fiber is quickly overcome on several occasions by the slightest pressures or inducements. Her will at times seems to be completely enslaved.

Her first repentance comes when Robin asks her to marry him: "I was now in a dreadful condition indeed, and now I repented heartily my easiness with the eldest brother; not from any reflection of conscience, for I was a stranger to those things, but I could not think of being a whore to one brother and a wife to the other."

Actually, Moll's repentance seems more like regret for having underestimated her chances for a better arrangement.

It is evident as the book unfolds that Moll has not been "led astray." She has very shrewdly calculated the course of her life. Throughout the story Moll considers or reflects on the path her life is taking. The occasion of Robin's marriage proposal causes Moll to say to the elder brother, "Upon serious consideration, for indeed now I began to consider things very seriously, and never till now I resolved to tell him of it." Again Moll considers what to do when she realizes she is not as bad as the people living in the Mint. She says, "I was not wicked enough for such fellows as these yet. On the contrary, I began to consider here very seriously what I had to do; how things stood with me, and what course I ought to take."

When the gentleman at Bath rejects any further contact with Moll, she reports "I cast about innumerable ways for my future state of life, and began to consider very seriously what I should do, but nothing offered."

After her Lancashire husband leaves and Moll is back in London alone she says that "here being perfectly alone, I had leisure to sit down and reflect seriously upon the last seven months' ramble I had made, . . ." After she is delivered of another baby and receives a letter from her London bank clerk saying he wants to see her again Moll is "exceedingly surprised at the news, and began now seriously to reflect on my present circumstances, . . ." She appears to reproach herself just before she marries him: "Then it occurred to me, 'What an abominable creature am I! and how is this innocent gentleman going to be abused by me!' How little does he think, that having divorced a whore, he is throwing himself into the arms of another!"

Nevertheless, she marries him and after his death begins her criminal career. As can be noted, many of her partial repentances dissipate into further scheming. Ironically Moll's energies are too consumed in maneuvering herself out of a bad situation to worry seriously about saving her soul.

When Moll is first committed to Newgate she makes the following statement: "Then I repented heartily of all my life past, but that repentance yielded me no satisfaction, no peace,

no, not in the least, because, as I said to myself, it was repenting
after the power of further sinning was taken away. I seemed
not to mourn that I had committed such crimes, and for the fact,
as it was an offense against God and my neighbour, but that I
was to be punished for it. I was penitent , as I thought, not that
I had sinned, but that I was to suffer and this took away all the
comforts of my repentance in my own thoughts."

This passage clearly shows another shallow repentance by
Moll. She fears not for her spiritual state but for her physical
being.

Even during her stay in Newgate, Moll does not appear to
really repent until quite some time after her talk with the pastor.
And perhaps even then Moll is really worried about being
hanged. The very fact that she insists on securing her inheritance
shows how the possession of earthly goods has much deeper
meaning for Moll than does the acquisition of spiritual well-
being. In fact, we see a meaningful contrast between Moll's
character and that of the governess, a former crook who seemingly has truly repented.

Note that the tears Moll weeps from time to time are
merely an emotional release rather than a sign of true repentance,
for even after the shedding her heart quickly hardens against
her victims and she continues their victimization. This is shown,
for example, when she steals the bundle from the burning house.
Whatever regret Moll has is weak indeed: "with all my sense
of its being cruel and inhuman, I could never find in my heart
to make any restitution."

Hardening

The question as to whether Moll ever really becomes a
hardened criminal is an interesting one. We have seen that,
motivated by greed, she has been able to commit the crassest of
criminal acts. But Defoe still reveals to us sentimental aspects
of Moll's personality that we cannot ignore. To say that she is a
thief with a soul is to credit her with more depth than Defoe
really shows us. We never really see Moll's inner life that completely. Yet it is evident that Defoe meant us to sympathize
with Moll; and we are able to sympathize with her because he
portrays her as a very likeable woman, who, despite her thieving
and prostitution,is well-liked by her contemporaries, and seems
to like them as well.

Defoe uses irony ingeniously in the passages telling us of Moll's thoughts during her various crimes. He often portrays her as moralistic; for example, when she steals the necklace from the child in Aldersgate Street, she feels she is actually doing the child a favor: "The thought of this booty put out all the thoughts of the first, and the reflections I had made wore quickly off; poverty, as I have said, hardened my heart, and my own necessities made me regardless of anything. The last affair left no great concern upon me, for as I did the poor child no harm, I only said to myself, I had given the parents a reproof for their negligence in leaving the poor little lamb to come home by itself, and it would teach them to take more care of it another time." Defoe didn't want us to condone the action and condemn the parents. Through ironic humor he gives us insight into Moll's attempts to rationalize her felonies.

Frequently Moll feels remorse—but it is a hollow remorse, for it neither leads her to curtail the particular crime she is bemoaning, nor does it prompt her to offer restitution. This is shown in her robbery of a woman whose house is on fire: "This was the greatest and the worst prize that ever I was concerned in; for indeed, though, as I have said above, I was hardened now beyond the power of all reflection in other cases, yet it really touched me to the very soul when I looked into this treasure, to think of the poor disconsolate gentlewoman who had lost so much by the fire. . . ."

Moll is shown as most compassionate in her relationships with her various lovers and husbands. She seems to truly love the elder brother. And when she marries his brother Robin, poor Robin never learns of the affair. Her second spouse is a rake, but she treats him well and helps him escape from his creditors. She nurses her men when they are sick and loves them when they are well. Her relationship with Jemmy seems to be full of love and compassion. Moll is in Newgate, under sentence of death, but when she learns Jemmy is there too her remorse and sense of guilt are genuine. "I was overwhelmed with grief for him; my own case gave me no disturbance compared to this, and I loaded myself with reproaches on his account." Moll is an ambivalent character. She is a criminal—but a sympathetic one. Her life of crime is constantly colored by her good humor, compassion and sense of loyalty.

CHARACTER SKETCHES

MAJOR CHARACTERS

Moll's Mother

Moll's mother was first mentioned in Chapter 1 as a young girl in Newgate Prison about to be hanged for a petty theft. She was saved because she was carrying a child (Moll), and was later transported to the colonies, leaving the one-and-a-half-year-old Moll in bad hands.

She appeared again in Chapter 8 now living in Virginia and the mother of Moll's husband. She reminisced to Moll about her experiences in Newgate Prison and Moll discovered that she was in actuality her own mother. This friendly, outgoing woman tried to convince Moll to remain married to her son (Moll's brother) in order to keep the family intact. When she died, she left some money and her plantation to Moll.

Moll Flanders

Moll, the heroine of the book, was born in Newgate Prison and abandoned at about a year-and-a-half. She was a forceful, persistent, resolute young girl who obtained her way in most things. She was attractive and so vain about her appearance that she was easily convinced men were in love with her.

Moll often moralized about her fear of poverty, her greed, her increasing hardness of heart, her criminal activities, her numerous husbands and lovers. Her evolving theory was that if England had provided properly for orphans she would not have fallen into bad hands and thus needed to fend for herself before she could be trained to make her way honestly in the world. According to her theory, a young girl in poor circumstances had the right to find support as best she could. Moll, vain and fearful of poverty, pursued her goal of obtaining security in life.

One aspect of this determination was Moll's drive to marry a rich man. A second aspect was her ruthless pursuit of money.

The result of the acts she performed to achieve these goals was the transformation of a beautiful innocent young girl into a hardened middle-aged criminal who was finally captured and sent to Newgate Prison. Her resourcefulness and conniving brought her release from prison and her transportation to Virginia. There, with Jemmy, her favorite husband, she was able to become, in a year's time, a wealthy plantation-owner. Throughout the novel we see Moll's dual nature—a penitent woman reproaching herself for her misdeeds, and a ruthless pursuer of ill-gotten wealth.

The Elder Brother

The elder son of the rich matron who took Moll into her household after the death of Moll's nurse was a gay, handsome man-about-town who contrived to seduce Moll through compliments, promises to marry her, and gifts of money. Later, he ended his relationship with Moll by virtually pushing her into a marriage with his younger brother, Robin.

Robin

Robin, the younger brother in the household, was good and open in his affections for Moll. Although he distressed his family by his love of the beautiful but penniless Moll, in the end he convinced his mother of the sincerity of his love. He later married Moll, with the help and encouragement of the elder brother, who wanted to be rid of her. Robin died after only five years of married life with Moll.

The Draper

The draper, an unprincipled gentleman, was described as "a tradesman that was rake, gentleman, shopkeeper, and beggar, all together." He became Moll's second husband and spent much of her money on extravagances for them. Because he continued to buy handsome things even when his money ran out, the draper's creditors had him imprisoned. He eventually escaped and went to France, telling Moll to consider him dead.

Moll's Brother

Moll's third husband, her brother, she married by mistake. He had been led to believe that Moll had a fortune; on discovering that she had no money, he suggested they go to Virginia to live on his plantation with his mother. When Moll found out that she was his sister and therefore wanted to leave him, he became ill and despondent. When, near the end of the book, Moll went back to Virginia, her brother was sick and nearly blind. He died within a year or so, never knowing of Moll's return.

The Gentleman of Bath

This gentleman became Moll's provider. Later they were lovers, and Moll had a baby boy by him. After six years of living as husband and wife, the gentleman became ill in the home of his wife's relatives. When he recovered, he abandoned Moll.

Jemmy

Jemmy was Moll's Lancashire husband. Although he deceived her into believing he had property because he thought *she* was wealthy, he actually loved her. He was an attractive, good-natured highwayman who landed in prison at the same time as Moll. She later arranged for him to be transported to Virginia with her and repaid his good humor with gifts and a home.

Bank Clerk

Moll described the bank clerk as "a quiet, sensible, sober man; virtuous, modest, sincere, and in his business diligent and just." When his wife ran away with another man, the bank clerk divorced her and married Moll. They lived together contentedly for five years. When he made a bad investment and lost a good deal of money, he became ill and died.

Moll's Son

This son was born to Moll of her marriage to her brother. He was loving toward Moll and only too happy to give her her inheritance as well as many gifts. He was a prosperous plantation-owner who was overjoyed to see his mother.

The Governess

The governess was a pickpocket, midwife, and procuress before Moll met her. As a midwife she was kind to Moll. Later she became a pawnbroker and Moll's partner in crime, pushing her into deeper and deeper criminal activities. She later became remorseful and discontinued her criminal pursuits; but she remained Moll's friend through all her trials in prison and in America.

MINOR CHARACTERS

The nurse was Moll's foster mother, whom the town authorities had made a guardian of orphans. She was a poor gentlewoman who was described as very religious, sober, pious, housewifely, clean, mannerly, and genteel. She operated a school where she taught housekeeping and sewing to poor orphans so that when they become old enough, they could find employment in the homes of the rich. She was very kind to Moll and employed her as an assistant so she wouldn't be sent into service.

The captain's widow met Moll while they were both hiding from their creditors in the Mint, a poor part of town. She invited Moll to live at her home in another part of town, saying that there Moll would perhaps meet a captain of a ship and marry him. Instead the captain's widow was the lucky one.

The north-country woman, through deceit and conniving, arranged for Moll to marry Jemmy, who she pretended was her brother. Actually she and Jemmy were ex-lovers, and both thought Moll had money.

The baronet met Moll when he was quite drunk, and she robbed him. Subsequently the two had an affair for about a year.

The minister was Moll's spiritual adviser while she was in Newgate Prison. He managed to get her sentence changed from hanging to transportation to the colonies. During his talks with Moll, he finally helped bring about her repentance.

The captain of the ship which transported Moll and Jemmy to America was friendly and easy to bribe. He made the long voyage pleasant by providing Moll and Jemmy with the comforts of first-class travelers.

In addition, there were many other characters, mostly unnamed, who had passing influence on the life of Moll Flanders.

CRITICAL OPINIONS

The various incidents in the eventful life of Moll Flanders, from the time of her seduction to that of her becoming a convict and a quiet settler in Maryland, are those of real life, as exemplified by multitudes of individuals who have run the career of their vicious propensities. The artless disposition of the narrative, the lively interest excited by unlooked for coincidences, the rich natural painting, the moral reflections, are all so many proofs of the knowledge and invention of the writer; but the facts were furnished him by the annals of Newgate. . . . From the character of the incidents that compose the present narrative, DeFoe was fully aware of the objectives that would be urged against it by the scrupulous. To conceal a single fact, would have taken so much from the fidelity of the portrait; all that he could do, therefore, was to neutralize the poison, by furnishing the strongest antidotes. Accordingly whilst he paints the courses of an everyday profligate in their natural colours, he shows us with the same faithfulness their natural tendency; and that, first or last, vice is sure to bring down its own punishment. His villains never prosper; but either come to an untimely end, or are brought to be penitents. In dressing up the present story, he tells us he had taken care to exclude everything that might be offensive; but conscious that he had a bad subject to work upon, he endeavours to interest the reader in the reflections arising out of it, that the moral might be more enticing than the fable.

> Walter Wilson, *Memoirs of the Life and Times of Daniel Defoe,* vol. III, 1830.

Of these novels we may, nevertheless, add, for the satisfaction of the inquisitive reader, that "Moll Flanders" is utterly vile and detestable: Mrs. Flanders was evidently born in sin. The best parts are the account of her childhood, which is pretty and affecting; the fluctuation of her feelings between remorse and hardened impenitence in Newgate; and the incident of her leading off the horse from the inn-door, though she had no place to put it in after she had stolen it.

> William Hazlitt, "Wilson's Life and Times of Daniel Defoe," *Edinburgh Review* (1830).

Deals with the sore of society in very much the spirit of M. Zola and his followers. Defoe lays bare the career of an abandoned woman, concealing nothing, extenuating nothing, but also hoping nothing. It could only be when inspired by the hope of amelioration, that such a narrative could be endurable. But Defoe's novel is inspired merely by hope of the good sale which of course it achieved: the morbid way in which he, like M. Zola, lingers over disgusting detail, and the perfunctory manner in which any necessary pieces of morality are introduced preclude us from attributing any moral purpose to a vivid and clever, but most revolting novel.

> P. F. Rowland, *A Comparison, Criticism and Estimate of the English Novelists from 1700 to 1850,* 1894.

Spiritual autobiography pursued thematic coherence amid or despite narrative incoherence: incoherence, that is, measured by the more rigorous standards of plotting which the novel was to evolve. So long as the protagonist's inward vicissitudes obeyed the traditional pattern, either of growth or decay, and so long as individual episodes contributed to this pattern with some consistency, an autobiography might be regarded as structually sound. Within such a convention, whose rationale lay in religious psychology rather than aesthetics, a logic of spiritual change within the character took precedence over a logic of outward action; within such a convention, discrete, apparently random episodes might be held to possess a unity both sufficient and meaningful. This convention, it seems to me, illuminates some basic features of the action and characterization of *Moll Flanders.*

> G. A. Starr, *Defoe: Spiritual Autobiography,* 1965.

No doubt *Moll Flanders* (first published on January 27, 1722) has its dull passages, but I would disagree that many can be found in that part of the book which tells of her life as a London Thief. Here, a different voice seems to be speaking. She divulges to Defoe, rather flatly and cold-bloodedly at times, as many different thieving techniques as she can remember. The result is very much the sort of thing he would have taken down in shorthand (at which he was skilled according to his own statement) during a series of interviews with a typical Newgate woman. Who could she have been?

> Gerald Howson, "Who Was Moll Flanders?" *The Times Literary Supplement,* January 18, 1968.

STUDY QUESTIONS

1. The single event that decisively launches the action in *Moll Flanders* is Moll's
   a. declaration to live well.
   b. seduction by the elder brother.
   c. orphanhood.

2. The one personality trait of Moll that Defoe most especially emphasizes is her
   a. vanity.
   b. beauty.
   c. gullibility.

3. Between the ages of eight and fourteen, Moll develops a strong obsession about being a
   a. chambermaid.
   b. prostitute.
   c. gentlewoman.

4. Moll's ambitions are thwarted because of
   a. her pride and vanity.
   b. the discrepancy between her genteel attainments and her real prospects in the world.
   c. her misunderstanding of the word "gentlewoman."

5. Recurring throughout the novel are evidences of Moll's
   a. momentary qualms and incomplete repentances.
   b. motherly concern for her children.
   c. reserve.

6. Moll marries the London bank clerk
   a. because she is in love with him.
   b. as part of her plan to obtain security.
   c. in order to steal his money.

7. Soon after the delivery of her son by her Lancashire lover, Moll receives a letter from her
   a. governess.
   b. husband-brother.
   c. London bank clerk.

8. The person from her past whom Moll meets in Newgate is
   a. her mother.

    b. Jemmy.

    c. her friend from the Mint.

9. Moll's real repentance comes when she

    a. learns of her mother's death.

    b. talks to the minister while in prison.

    c. realizes that she has finally been captured and incarcerated.

10. When Moll returns to the colonies, she is unusually affected by the sight of her

    a. brother.

    b. son.

    c. mother.

ANSWERS: 1-b; 2-a; 3-c; 4-b; 5-a; 6-b; 7-c; 8-b; 9-b; 10-b.

1. Briefly describe at least five episodes which illustrate Moll's pseudo-repentance.

2. Show that Moll's ambition to become a gentlewoman is not a mere whimsical desire.

3. Show how Moll's conscience, a weak and faltering guide, is overcome on crucial occasions by external pressures or inducements.

4. Trace the gradual hardening of Moll's character prior to her final repentance.

5. Explain what sort of shady activities Moll was engaged in before she began her actual career in crime.

BIBLIOGRAPHY

Allen, Walter. *Six Great Novelists: Defoe, Fielding, Scott, Dickens, Stevenson, Conrad.* London: Jamish Hamilton, 1955.

Defoe, Daniel. *Moll Flanders.* Afterword by Kenneth Rexroth. New York: The New American Library, 1964.

Donoghue, Denis. "The Values of Moll Flanders," *Sewanee Review,* LXXI (Spring, 1963), pp. 287–303.

Fitzgerald, Brian. *Daniel Defoe: A Study in Conflict.* Chicago: Henry Regenery Company, 1955.

Howson, Gerald. "Who Was Moll Flanders?," *Times Literary Supplement, 3438* (January 18, 1968), pp. 63–64.

Hunter, J. Paul. *The Reluctant Pilgrim.* Baltimore: The John Hopkins Press, 1966.

Koonce, Howard L. "Moll's Muddle: Defoe's Use of Irony in *Moll Flanders,*" *The Journal of English Literary History,* XXX (December, 1963), pp. 378–79.

Lovell, Robert Morss and Hughes, Helen Sard. *The History of the Novel in England.* New York: Houghton Mifflin, 1932.

McCullough, Bruce. *Representative English Novelists: Defoe to Conrad.* New York: Harper and Brothers, 1946.

Moore, John Robert. *Daniel Defoe, Citizen of the Modern World.* Chicago: University of Chicago Press, 1958.

Novak, Maximillian. "The Problem of Necessity in Defoe's Fiction," *Philogical Quarterly,* XL (October, 1961), pp. 513–24.

Rowland, P. F. *A Comparison, Criticism and Estimate of the English Novelists from 1700 to 1850,* 1894.

Secord, Arthur Wellesley. *Studies in the Narrative Method of Defoe.* New York: Russell and Russell, Inc., 1963.

Starr, G. A. *Defoe: Spiritual Autobiography.* Princeton, New Jersey: Princeton University Press, 1965.

Sutherland, James. *Defoe.* London: Methuen, 1937.

Watson, Francis. *Daniel Defoe.* London: Longmans, Green and Company, 1952.

Watt, Ian. *The Rise of the Novel: Studies in Defoe, Richardson and Fielding.* Berkeley and Los Angeles: University of California Press, 1957.

Wilson, Walter. *Memoirs of the Life and Times of Daniel Defoe.* 1830.